'Increasingly anthropologists work outside academia with or for corporations, and must collaborate with others in the corporation – with management, vendors and consumers of differing orientations. In this, ethnographers encounter new frames of knowledge, deal with power relations and get caught up in emotional quandaries. This volume wonderfully illustrates the kinds of entanglements business anthropologists routinely encounter in their work. The range of authors presented here will be especially helpful to business anthropologists, students, marketers and consumer researchers, offering diverse perspectives for understanding consuming culture.'
Timothy de Waal Malefyt, *Fordham University School of Business, USA*

'*Collaborative Ethnography in Business Environments* is one of those rare edited volumes we should all have on our shelf. Maryann McCabe treats us to an eloquent analysis of knowledge, power and emotion in collaborative work, interwoven with examples from her own considerable experience. The masterful and beautifully written introduction alone would make the volume a must-have for scholars and students, but its *coup de grâce* is that the authors gathered together in this volume are established names working at the intersection of anthropology and business.'
Patricia Sunderland, Practica, LLC; co-editor of
Handbook of Anthropology in Business

T0359085

Collaborative Ethnography in Business Environments

In a global and rapidly changing commercial environment, businesses increasingly use collaborative ethnographic research to understand what motivates their employees and what their customers value. In this volume, anthropologists, marketing professionals, computer scientists and others examine issues, challenges and successes of ethnographic cooperation in the corporate world. The book

- argues that constant shifts in the global marketplace require increasing multidisciplinary and multicultural teamwork in consumer research and organizational culture;
- addresses the need of corporate ethnographers to be adept at reading and translating the social constructions of knowledge and power, in order to contribute to the team process of engaging research participants, clients and stakeholders;
- reveals the essentially dynamic process of collaborative ethnography;
- shows how multifunctional teams design and carry out research, communicate findings and implications for organizational objectives, and craft strategies to achieve those objectives to increase the vibrancy of economies, markets and employment rates worldwide.

Maryann McCabe is a Senior Lecturer at the University of Rochester, USA, and Founder and Principal of Cultural Connections, LLC.

Collaborative Ethnography in Business Environments

Edited by Maryann McCabe

Routledge
Taylor & Francis Group

LONDON AND NEW YORK

Originally published in 2014 as a thematic issue of the *International Journal of Business Anthropology*, vol. 5(1), ISSN 2155-6237

First published 2017
by Routledge
2 Park Square, Milton Park, Abingdon, Oxon OX14 4RN

and by Routledge
711 Third Avenue, New York, NY 10017

Routledge is an imprint of the Taylor & Francis Group, an informa business

British Library Cataloguing-in-Publication Data
A catalogue record for this book is available from the British Library

Library of Congress Cataloging-in-Publication Data
Names: McCabe, Maryann, editor.
Title: Collaborative ethnography in business environments / edited by Maryann McCabe.
Description: Abingdon, Oxon ; New York, NY : Routledge, 2016. | "Originally published in 2014 as a thematic issue of the International Journal of Business Anthropology, vol. 5(1), ISSN 2155-6237." | Includes bibliographical references and index.
Identifiers: LCCN 2016006618| ISBN 9781138691599 (hardback : alk. paper) | ISBN 9781138691544 (pbk. : alk. paper) | ISBN 9781315534572 (ebook)Subjects: LCSH: Business anthropology. | Corporate culture.
Classification: LCC GN450.8 .C65 2016 | DDC 302.3/5--dc23
LC record available at http://lccn.loc.gov/2016006618

ISBN: 978-1-138-69159-9 (hbk)
ISBN: 978-1-138-69154-4 (pbk)
ISBN: 978-1-315-53457-2 (ebk)

Typeset in Sabon
by Saxon Graphics Ltd, Derby

To Owen M. Lynch (1931–2013),
a scholar of India,
devoted to improving the lives of Dalits,
and beloved by his students.

Contents

Notes on contributors

Russell Belk is the Kraft Foods Canada Chair in Marketing, York University, Schulich School of Business. He has a Ph.D. in marketing from the University of Minnesota.

Robin Beers is Senior Vice President, Wells Fargo Bank, Wholesale Internet Services, Customer Experience Insights, and earned her Ph.D. in organizational psychology from Alliant International University – San Francisco Bay.

Elizabeth K. Briody, Founder and Principal of Cultural Keys, LLC, has a Ph.D. in anthropology from the University of Texas at Austin.

Ken C. Erickson is Clinical Faculty Member, University of South Carolina, Moore College of Business. He has a Ph.D. in anthropology from the University of Kansas.

Alice D. Peinado is Director of Education, Instituto Marangoni School of Fashion, Paris. She is a Ph.D. candidate at Ecole d'Hautes Etudes des Sciences Sociales.

Mary Ann Sprague is Research Ethnographer, Palo Alto Research Center (PARC), Work Practice & Technology Group, Xerox. She has an M.S. in computer science from the Rochester Institute of Technology.

Margaret H. Szymanski is Senior Researcher, Palo Alto Research Center (PARC), Work Practice & Technology Group, Xerox. She earned a Ph.D. at the University of California at Santa Barbara.

Inga Treitler, Founder and Principal of Anthropology Imagination, LLC., has a Ph.D. in anthropology from the University of Illinois at Urbana-Champaign.

Patricia Wall is Research Manager, Palo Alto Research Center (PARC), Work Practice & Technology Group, Xerox. She has an M.S. in psychology from North Carolina State University.

Jennifer Watts-Englert is Senior Cognitive Engineer, Palo Alto Research Center (PARC), Work Practice & Technology Group, Xerox. She has a Ph.D. in cognitive engineering from Ohio State University.

1 Introduction: Collaborative ethnography

Intersection of knowledge, power and emotion

Maryann McCabe

The title of a novel, *Fieldwork*, perched on the library shelf, captured my attention (Berlinski 2007). The book tells the fascinating story of Martiya, a young anthropologist from UC Berkeley who goes to Thailand to conduct doctoral research among Thai hill tribes and later returns to live there. Living with the same people is a US missionary whose family has worked to convert the people to Christianity for many years. When the missionary converts Martiya's lover, a local man, and as a result the lover leaves her, Martiya kills the missionary. This is a novel. Convicted of murder, Martiya ends up in prison where she writes brilliant ethnographies. The novel, written by a US journalist who had plied his trade in Thailand, is based on the conversion to Christianity of the Lisu people of northern Thailand studied by anthropologist Paul Durrenberger (1989).

I refer to this story because it brings to the fore issues concerning collaboration and crossing boundaries. Martiya erases the boundary between her culture and Thai culture by returning to live with the hill tribe after completing her doctoral work and becoming one of them. The missionary, on the other hand, maintains the boundary by demanding that the people leave their culture and adopt a Christian life. In the world of business anthropology, ethnographers are faced with finding ways to cross boundaries without going to the extremes recounted in the novel of either effacing or rigidly adhering to boundaries. In fact, business anthropologists position themselves as adept at crossing cultural boundaries and collaborating (Brun-Cottan 2010; Briody 2013). The authors in this volume address roles that business anthropologists assume as choreographers or participants in collaborative ethnography when they work in and with corporations and other organizations. Such roles are challenging because they involve the intersection of different sources of knowledge, power and emotion. Since knowledge, power and emotion are social constructions, they require reading and translation when people work together. The entanglements of knowledge, power and emotion make ethnographic collaboration a dynamic and changing process of social interaction.

Martiya's story resides at a particular intersection of knowledge, power and emotion, but the outcome of her fictional narrative thankfully differs from results of ethnographic collaboration in business anthropology. For Martiya, the result was her death and destruction of the traditional lifeway of a people. Like Martiya, business anthropologists engage in ethnographic research, but they collaborate with multidisciplinary and multifunctional teams that design and carry out research, communicate findings and implications for organizational objectives, and craft strategies to achieve those objectives. At stake is the success of individual projects and from larger perspective the vibrancy of economies, markets and employment rates worldwide.

Knowledge

Collaborative ethnography involves different sources of knowledge in the design, implementation and use of research. The conception of knowledge in postmodern anthropology has altered with the insight from Edward Said's work that knowledge is situated in time and space (Said 1979) and the observation in Michel Foucault's writings on power and subjugated knowledges that we must speak about knowledge in the plural (Foucault 1980). When different kinds of knowledge meet, put forward by persons collaborating on research, how is the learning combined and what does the new intellectual form produce?

Each knowledge provides a partial truth. Together, various forms of knowledge may offer a fuller picture, though not a complete view of a given context. Anthropologists Edwards and Petrovic-Steger, in a volume paying tribute to Marilyn Strathern, describe the melding of different sources of knowledge as recombinant knowledge (2011: 4). This metaphor, *recombinant knowledge*, is powerful because its biological roots refer to creating something novel; in the recombinant DNA case, it means bringing together genetic material from different species and creating molecular sequences that would not otherwise exist in organisms. In relation to business anthropologists working collaboratively, recombinant knowledge opens up other ways of understanding and lets us ask different questions and seek solutions in new directions. For example, in my experience working on a multidisciplinary team with engineers to design a sustainable mass transportation system, the engineers looked at technical design while the anthropologists looked at consumer transportation practices. Together we framed the project with the question, how could we design a sustainable mass transportation system that people would use? The framing gave us a more holistic view representing technical as well as human needs and constraints.

Recombinant knowledge does not happen automatically, however, when people talk about business projects from their particular disciplinary or functional vantage. Simple exposure to another's way of interpreting may be insufficient for opening the eyes of fellow collaborators. Yet, as anthropologist Marietta Baba and her colleagues (2004) point out, cognitive convergence must occur in order for collaborators to communicate effectively. As they write, "It means suspending our own judgment as we learn the cultural logic and rationality of others' divergent beliefs and values, while also allowing those others to call our own beliefs and values into question as they learn about us" (2004: 583). Thus, the notion of collaboration involves the epistemological and arguably ontological issues of grasping different sets of cultural categories.

Shared understanding requires translation across boundaries in order to comprehend issues at hand, such as business models and practices, customer segmentation models, environmental constraints and so forth. Sources of knowledge become validated externally through scientific or non-scientific means, including personal experience and social interaction. By reading and translating other perspectives, anthropologists engage in the art of persuasion. They play a double role shifting back and forth between participation and observation (Favret-Saada 1990). Comfortable leaving their anthropological moorings, they can make explicit the tacit cultural assumptions underlying information placed on the table by other collaborators. In this sense, business anthropologists live in liminal space because they make sense of different kinds of knowledge and encourage or persuade others to look at the meanings being unearthed.

When perspectival understanding occurs, more productive working relationships can ensue. For instance, in the transportation project mentioned above, the anthropologists were initially put off by the concept of externalities because it seemed to dismiss human factors in technical design. However, when the anthropologists plumbed the meaning of externalities with the engineers, they found that the concept refers to costs and benefits, such as air pollution and public safety, that affect a party who did not choose to incur the cost or benefit. The engineers affirmed the influence of human factors in technical design and welcomed input from the anthropologists.

Power

Collaborative relationships implicate power because of asymmetries among persons working together which shape their joint endeavors. A source of power for business anthropologists, arising from the ability to represent the ethnographic other, is contingent on evolving and changing positionality among collaborators. Postmodern anthropology recognizes that anthropological authority no longer rests on the privileged position of colonial times (Marcus and Fischer 1986), and more recent research efforts aim to let ethnographic subjects assert their own voice, especially in applied and advocacy work (Cook 2009). In the collaborative environment, greater inclusion of the other expands to include not only study subjects but also stakeholders who wish to influence the design, implementation and use of ethnographic research.

Business anthropologists, whether consultants or organizational employees, do not typically hold positions of high power in relation to the organization which is undertaking collaborative ethnography. In the hierarchy of control, persons with superior ranking in the organization typically have final say. Sometimes it is even necessary to assert the anthropological voice in collaborative exchange (Wasson 2000; Denny 2013). Based on my experience as practitioner, the anthropologist's expertise in cultural analysis is most often welcome and appreciated. However, it is sometimes contested because meaning in collaborative contexts is mediated through different lenses (Malefyt 2003). For example, when I was conducting collaborative ethnography for a pizza company, corporate managers participating on the research team were initially reluctant to accept some of the research findings because the findings conflated the reigning model of market segmentation at the company. It took many conversations for the client to realize that their previously developed model of market segments or types of moms did not capture the everyday reality of mothers organizing family pizza nights. Market segmentations are abstractions that can hinder grasp of actual consumption practices (Sunderland and Denny 2011).

Collaborative ethnography in and with organizations makes the research process transparent to participants on the project team. Transparency occurs by definition (Lassiter 2005). As Lassiter writes, *collaborative ethnography* is "an approach to ethnography that deliberately and explicitly emphasizes collaboration at every point in the ethnographic process, without veiling it – from project conceptualization, to fieldwork, through the writing process" (2005: xx). This transparency reveals a tension for business anthropologists insofar as they are accountable to the subjects of their ethnographic work and to productive processes concerning design, marketing and organizational change (Cefkin 2009). When potential conflict emerges in the tension between responsibility to research subjects and to corporate goals, business anthropologists must resolve any dilemmas that pose threats to their professional ethics, including the injunction of doing no harm to study participants and obtaining informed consent (Fluehr-Lobban 2013). In the transparent process of working together, other team members can usually comprehend the ethical issues, and resolution occurs even though it may take time to achieve (Gluesing 2014). It helps for collective sights to remain focused on the goal of gaining ethnographic insight through cultural analysis.

Emotion

The entanglement of emotion in collaborative ethnography deepens the challenge of working together and trying to share knowledge and negotiate power relations. Collaboration can raise intense emotions because project stakes run high and professionals cherish the theories and methods of their own particular fields. As Squires and Byrne (2002) note, team participants "must constantly break free of the most cherished individual, professional, and cultural perceptions" (2002: xv). Otherwise, for example, outbursts of anger and superiority can erode a sense of others being worthwhile team members capable of contributing to the engagement. More careful expression and acceptance of feelings may orient projects to fruitful completion instead of disengaged failure.

Like knowledge and power, emotion is a social construction. It develops in context and involves the cultural appraisal and moral judgment of situations (Lynch 1990). Based on a study of collaboration in an Austrian company, Krawinkler (2013) finds that trust is a critical yet culture-bound success factor in corporate life. People do not walk onto teams with blind trust but with *emic* ideas about trustworthiness so that establishing trust relations is "an evolving process where experiences are constantly checked against expectations" (2013: 161). For example, if a team member completes a task that he or she promised to do, other team members are likely to make a positive assessment of the person's trustworthiness. When people come to trust each other in collaborative settings, a favorable milieu for validating sources of knowledge brought by other team members comes into existence.

The difficulty of negotiating entanglements of emotion in collaborative ethnography is matched by the reward of doing so. For example, a study I recently conducted for a French company brought me into collaboration with a psychologist, a known and trusted colleague. Although the psychologist agreed with my analysis of employee satisfaction in terms of power and hierarchical relationships at the company, the psychologist wanted to speak about employee experiences in terms of universal human truths and a psychological model of development across the life cycle. My initial feeling was hostile, a resistance to the idea of universality in preference for explanation based on contextualization. Although my internal hostility ran high, we managed to find common ground in mapping the cultural meanings underlying employee concerns and aspirations onto specific stages of human needs and mastery of tasks. As it turned out, the collaborative result helped to make the analysis more comprehensible to company team members. Corporate managers could understand and appreciate employee issues when they thought about them as issues facing all human beings. In this case, intertwining anthropological and psychological concepts led the client to formulate human resource management strategies more responsive to employee expectations.

Contributions to this volume

The contributing authors deal with the entanglements of knowledge, power and emotion that business anthropologists face in collaborative ethnography. They speak about new roles and directions they are taking, working on teams and mediating worldviews, and the value of the holistic perspective. Issues and problems they encounter are illustrated with examples from their own work experience. Taken together, the chapters provide an inspiring account of current practice in collaborative ethnography with clients, stakeholders, and research participants.

In her chapter about companies facing the competitive pressures of a world that is exploding with change, **Robin Beers** explores the multiple roles ethnographic researchers assume within organizations. Beers argues that in addition to the traditional role of being purveyors of insight, ethnographic researchers can and must be knowledge brokers and change agents. The strategic imperative for companies to become more customer-centric means taking a holistic perspective on customers and employees. Organizational learning occurs when a company maps the customer journey of engagement with a product onto its own work processes, as customer touch-points traverse organizational silos and functional areas. Beers describes how the initiation of ethnographic research catalyzes cross-group collaboration when multifunctional teams analyze the fit, or lack thereof, between customer experience and company processes. An example of collaborative ethnography conducted at Wells Fargo Bank gives us an insider's view on dialogue that took place among people from different units at the bank. A multifunctional team was able to wade through ambiguity, translate terminology from different perspectives, and eventually develop alignment around a common purpose. This dialogue achieved shared understanding or recombinant knowledge. But, Beers points out, such conversations do not happen automatically. They have to be intentionally designed into collaborative research projects. This is where ethnographic researchers play multiple roles. Going beyond data collection, analysis and reporting, they can become knowledge brokers and change agents in organizations.

Elizabeth Briody and **Ken Erickson** discuss interactions among people working in large organizations with entrenched silos. There is such a tendency for people to align within their respective silos when faced with opportunities for innovation and demands for cross-silo interaction that the word *silo* stands metaphorically for difficulty and dysfunction. The silo-ed organizations where the authors conducted ethnographic research are an intimate apparel company, an automotive firm, and a hospital. As they relate, cross-silo interactions can have different progressions and outcomes. The authors analyze the paths of cross-silo interactions in projects undertaken at these organizations. The projects ended in various states of success or failure. For example, an attempt to develop a global vehicle program among engineering units of the automotive firm foundered in difficulty when participants could not discuss and resolve different work practices and processes in each silo. In other words, they were unable to translate knowledge across silo boundaries. Failure ensued when units usurped power by going up their chains of command and over the head of the program manager to gain their way. In another example, a hospital was able to reduce patient wait time in the emergency room through organizational restructuring and successful collaboration among several hospital units. Based on analysis of all the research projects conducted at the three organizations, Briody and Erickson identify five cultural dimensions that are important to successful system-wide innovation. Key to innovation is collaboration among people working in different silos.

Based on their experience in a corporate research group at Xerox, **Jennifer Watts-Englert, Margaret Syzmanski, Patricia Wall** and **Mary Ann Sprague** write about methodology for engaging stakeholders in ethnographic research. Methods employed by the Xerox Innovation Group have evolved in response to financially hard times that require corporate researchers to locate funding through client partnerships, and in response to industry customers seeking to embrace alternative research methods. The authors define different types of stakeholders and describe five ways in which clients are included in ethnographic projects. The five ways involve increasing degrees of collaboration: advisory boards, field visits with subject matter experts, analytic data sessions, co-design in iterative research processes, and competency transfer. Case studies are used to illustrate these avenues for client participation. Involving clients in all phases of research creates transparency in the ethnographic process. The authors point out that taking stakeholders to the field is challenging and time intensive yet worthwhile. They discuss ways of dealing with emotions, establishing trust, and avoiding stakeholder interference in the field. Overall, the engagement of stakeholders leads to a radical shift in the way clients think about the utility of ethnographic methods. This is most salient in competency transfer where clients request training to gain proficiency in ethnographic skills. The authors have formalized an ethnographic certificate program for teaching ethnographic field methods so that clients can create self-sustaining work practice teams.

In her chapter, **Alice Peinado** takes a holistic view of customer experience from a design anthropology perspective. She argues that brand coherence requires moving beyond brand design as storytelling. Brands tell stories but they also create customer experience. Fixing customer problems often involves redesigning how a company does business. Rupture points in customer experience can result from dysfunction in management practices that warrant change in how services are delivered. An example from the banking and insurance industry highlights need for an anthropological approach to design that examines customer experience from this holistic point of view. In the example, customers encounter problems trying to repay loans because of limited collaboration between units within the company and across subcontractors. As a result, brand experience is fragmented, disjointed and incoherent. Peinado addresses the difficulties of trying to resolve organizational issues when working with clients on a consulting basis. Consultants usually work with an individual person or unit within a corporation, such as R&D or marketing, and consequently become embedded in the power relations of the organization. In the context of different and conflicting agendas within the company, it can be hard for the voice of the anthropologist to be heard. In addition, there may be reluctance or even inability on the part of the client (individual or unit) to address the organization-wide structure and change necessary to resolve problems that customers are experiencing. Nonetheless, Peinado contends that empathizing with the customer's world means checking the business set-up and being willing to engage in organizational transformation.

In his essay on videography, **Russell Belk** discusses the current state of ethnography and collaborative image making. He describes how our lives have become saturated with visual representations and how the current "born digital" generation expects visual images and becomes bored with textual information. Occurring alongside this rise of the image, Belk argues, is the crisis of representation and concern among anthropologists and ethnographic filmmakers with the unchallenged dominance of the author's voice. Belk looks at benefits and problems of opening visual ethnographic research to the voices of participants in consumer research. Giving cameras and camcorders to participants and asking them to provide a visual narrative of their lives empowers participants. In return, consumer researchers gain more naturalistic data and personal points of view that create a richer picture for clients than visually unaided presentation of research results. Newer technologies, such as smart phones and online collage applications, enhance this process of self-representation. Belk addresses the need to safeguard informant identity, which is more difficult to do in visual representations than textual representations, and he provides examples from his work of negotiating compromises with informants that protect their identity. He also talks about bias underlying self-representations posted on new media such as blogs, personal web pages and social media. His conclusion is that empowering subjects to engage in visual self-representation creates another truth, not a "truer" truth, but at least allowing ethnographers to learn how people wish to represent themselves.

Inga Treitler revisits the concept of participant observer and argues that the dichotomy between studying in a foreign society and in your own society is false. Subjectivity poses risks in both cases. Treitler shows how the risks can be managed in backyard ethnography. This is important for companies wanting to understand what matters to consumers in these changing times and to respond to new marketplace demands. Companies are increasingly seeking knowledge directly from customers by joining ethnographers in the field and even more directly by engaging with customers through interactive techniques such as social media and mobile apps. For Treitler, this type of collaborative ethnography casts the client and the customer as backyard ethnographers who, like anthropologists conducting research in their own society, have a large degree of cultural familiarity. Doing ethnography in one's own society, or metaphorically, one's comfort zone, generates upsides and downsides. On the upside, shared points of reference, such as local landmarks and personalities, create a sense of connection. However, on the downside, shared points of reference are not the same as shared experiences. Backyard ethnographers need to remain aware of the boundary or symbolic membrane between themselves and their research participants. For example, clients going to the field with an ethnographer may hold opinions about market segments and product users and feel a sense of ownership over the customer relationship. This can preclude allowing new perceptions outside the familiar box. Using material from interviews conducted in her community, Treitler provides tips for defamiliarizing participant observers working in their own backyard.

Conclusion

I thank the authors for their contributions to this volume. Their insights show how the process of collaborative ethnography is rooted in anthropology itself – crossing cultural boundaries and representing others. The authors demonstrate the value of the holistic perspective in negotiating different sources of knowledge, power and emotion when business anthropologists are working on teams. Their contributions to this volume provide new perspectives on the problems and benefits of engaging research participants, clients and stakeholders in collaborative ethnography.

References

Baba, M. L., J. Gluesing, H. Ratner & K. H. Wagner. (2004). The contexts of knowing: Natural history of a globally distributed team. *Journal of Organizational Behavior, 25*, 547–587.

Berlinski, M. (2007). *Fieldwork*. New York: Picador.

Briody, E. K. (2013). Collaboration and anthropology in corporate work. *Journal of Business Anthropology, 2*(2), 134–141.

Brun-Cottan, F. (2010). The anthropologist as ontological choreographer. In *Ethnography and the corporate encounter*, ed. M. Cefkin, New York: Berghahn, 158–181.

Cefkin, M. (2009). Introduction: Business, anthropology, and the growth of corporate ethnography. In *Ethnography and the corporate encounter*, ed. M. Cefkin, New York: Berghahn, 1–37.

Cook, S. R. (2009). The collaborative power struggle. *Collaborative Anthropologies, 2*, 109–114.

Denny, R. (2013). The cry of practicality. In *Advancing ethnography in corporate environments*, ed. B. Jordan, Walnut Creek, CA: Left Coast Press, 136–150.

Durrenberger, E. P. (1989). *Lisu religion*. Southeast Asia Publications Occasional Papers No.13. DeKalb: Northern Illinois University.

Edwards, J., & M. Petrovic-Steger. (2011). Introduction: On recombinant knowledge and debts that inspire. In *Recasting Anthropological knowledge: Inspiration and social science*, ed. J. Edwards and M. Petrovic-Steger, Cambridge: Cambridge University Press, 1–18.

Favret-Saada, J. (1990). About participation. *Culture, Medicine and Psychiatry, 14*(2), 189–199.

Fluehr-Lobban, C. (2013). *Ethics and anthropology: Ideas and practice*. Lanham, MD: AltaMira Press.

Foucault, M. (1980). *Power/Knowledge: Selected interviews and other writings 1972–1977*, ed. C. Gordon. New York: Vintage.

Gluesing, J. C. (2014). Ethical considerations in global multi-stakeholder work. *Journal of Business Anthropology*, Special Issue 1: Ethics in Business Anthropology, 79–95.

Krawinkler, S. A. (2013). *Trust is a choice: Prolegomena of anthropology of trust(s)*. Heidelberg, Germany: Carl-Auer Verlag.

Lassiter, L. E. (2005). *The Chicago guide to collaborative ethnography*. Chicago: University of Chicago Press.

Lynch, O. M. (1990). *Divine passions: The social construction of emotion in India*. Berkeley: University of California Press.

Malefyt, T. D. (2003). Models, metaphors and client relations: The negotiated meanings of advertising. In *Advertising Cultures*, ed. T.D. Malefyt and B. Moeran, Oxford: Berg, 139–163.

Marcus G. E., & M. M. J. Fischer. (1986). *Anthropology as cultural critique: An experimental moment in the human sciences*. Chicago: University of Chicago Press.

Said, E. W. (1979). *Orientalism*. New York: Vintage.

Squires, S., & B. Byrne. (2002). Introduction: The growing partnership between research and design. In *Creating breakthrough ideas: The collaboration of anthropologists and designers in the product development industry*, ed. S. Squires and B. Byrne, pp. xiii–xviii. Westport, CT: Bergin & Garvey.

Sunderland, P., & R. Denny. (2011). Consumer segmentation in practice: An ethnographic account of slippage. In *Inside marketing: Practices, ideologies, devices,* ed. D. Zwick and J. Cayla, Oxford: Oxford University Press, 137–161.

Wasson, C. (2000). Ethnography in the field of design. *Human Organization, 59*(4), 377–388.

2 Humanizing organizations

Researchers as knowledge brokers and change agents

Robin Beers

As business becomes more customer-centric, the need for insight increases

Competitive pressures and more empowered customers have made customer experience a critical strategic imperative for every industry and every company. The need for deep understanding about people, their experience, and how they define value has increased as businesses change to become more customer-centric:

> Imagine a crazy wonderland where most of what you learned in business school is either upside-down or backward – where customers control the company, jobs are avenues of self-expression, the barriers to competition are out of your control, strangers design your products, few features are better, advertising drives customers away, demographics are beside the point, whatever you sell you take back, and best practices are obsolete at birth; where meaning talks, money walks, and stability is a fantasy; where talent trumps obedience, imagination beats knowledge, and empathy trounces logic.
>
> (Neumeier, 2008, p. xx)

In today's disruptive economic and industrial landscape, incremental improvement leaves companies – and whole industries – vulnerable to competitive threats and total disintermediation. As customers become more connected and empowered, and traditional sources of competitive dominance no longer suffice, "the only sustainable competitive advantage is knowledge of and engagement with customers" (Cooperstein, 2013, p. xx).

Forrester Research calls this era of customer-focus "The Age of the Customer." *Humanize* authors Notter and Grant proclaim that in business "we have begun to witness a revival of the importance of being human" (2011, p. 3). And author and strategist, Nilofer Merchant, describes this as the "Social Era" where companies need to "take in market signals for what customers want, how they want it, where and when they should be able to get it, and how much they are willing to pay" (Merchant, 2012, Digital

Location: 405 of 1229). No matter which label we use, this is an era that requires companies get closer to people to understand how their current and potential customers define value.

Customer experience as a strategic imperative requires organizations to develop new capabilities

An organization's focus on customers heightens the need for insights about their opinions, needs, and experiences. Ethnographic research is particularly valuable for eliciting the deep, detailed, and nuanced understanding of what people do and why they do it that way. But user researchers who come from, and are trained in, ethnographic and design research perspectives can play a more significant role in organizations than merely bringing customer insights to the table; they can bring in new capabilities which originate specifically from their human-centered practices and world view.

Over the decade I've managed customer-insights teams at Wells Fargo Bank, the role and influence of researchers – particularly those with ethnographic and design research training and expertise – has expanded tremendously. We've gone from delivering quantitative and qualitative insights for discrete projects in a largely transactional fashion, to orchestrating and facilitating organizational change. My academic training in organizational psychology may make me particularly attuned to this evolution, but I have always felt that the true power of insights, particularly those from ethnographic research, lies in their ability to help organizations change course and achieve greater success by aligning more closely with customers and employees. To that end, I've always challenged the researchers on my teams to become great consultants, expert communicators, compelling storytellers, and strong facilitators, in addition to being researchers. In this chapter, I contend that researchers need to offer and organizations need to develop the following capabilities to thrive in today's complex and constantly changing milieu:

- Embracing a holistic mindset
- Creating shared understanding
- Engaging in design-oriented problem solving

These competencies are more than skills or tools; they are types of intelligence necessary to build human-centered organizations for today's networked world. In addition, dynamically changing environments call for the interpretation of new events and the re-interpretation of existing practices through learning (Boland, Tenkasi, & Te'eni, 1994). These abilities increase "organizational learning," or, the tactical- and cultural-adaptive capabilities of organizations to respond to market and environmental forces (Senge, 1990). Organizational learning creates the capacity to develop new, or adapt old, competencies and innovate (Brown & Duguid, 1991; Easterby-Smith, Snell, & Gherardi, 1998). In a customer-empowered, connected world exploding with change, businesses need to establish processes of reflection and learning to innovate. The capabilities described in this chapter can also help businesses mitigate the risks associated with becoming out of touch with customer expectations and achieve an overall increase in effective cross-functional collaboration and team efficacy.

To help businesses thrive while meeting customer needs and expectations, researchers must become more than purveyors of insight; they must also act as knowledge brokers and change agents. But to fully inhabit these roles, researchers need to expand their own capabilities to include design-thinking techniques, knowledge of organizational change models, and expert facilitation and consultation skills. This chapter describes how researchers bring value beyond insights by infusing organizations with new ways of seeing and working, as part of a broader user-centered design process, and illuminates the more expansive role researchers can play as a result.

Embracing a holistic mindset for problem solving

In intermittently changing environments like the ones we now inhabit, a holistic perspective is critical for understanding both how things work and the underlying dynamics that tell us why. Today's organizations need insight into the entire customer lifecycle and help connecting the dots between siloed organizational departments. Ethnographers, as observers and interpreters of cultural systems, are accustomed and trained to look at systems holistically, to consider the entire ecosystem, or context, and not just the small piece that is impacted by a particular product or service. Holism maintains that the entirety equals more than its parts and contains properties that cannot be discovered through the analysis of parts. It stands in contrast with a reductionist worldview.

Since the Industrial Era, most traditional corporations have operated out of a reductionist, mechanistic mindset. This way of thinking seeks to control complexity by breaking systems into smaller pieces in order to maximize efficiency. It works best in stable, routine, predictable environments. Mechanistic organizations typically rely on role specialization, with each function acting like parts of a machine, each doing the job they are meant to do but not much more. We are no longer living in this world. However, many organization structures still reflect Industrial Era assumptions and we often lack embedded work practices that help us to see whole systems (Notter & Grant, 2011, pp. 132–134).

Forrester Research coined the term "customer experience ecosystem" to describe the complex system of people (employees, partners and customers), products, services, technologies, and touchpoints that when examined as a whole, constitute the holistic customer experience (Bodine, 2013). Organizations need tools, such as customer journey maps, to help them view and understand their ecosystem and the customer's journey through it (see Figure 2.1).

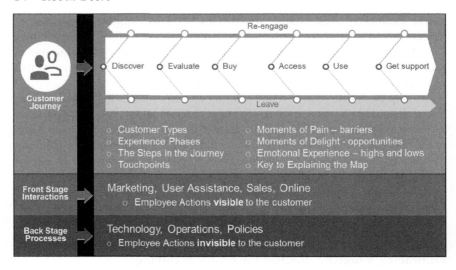

Figure 2.1 This generic customer journey map shows the range of data depicted, including steps, touchpoints, pain points, and emotions.

Ethnographers working in business are poised to bring the benefits of holistic, systems thinking to their companies through mapping the end-to-end customer, and sometimes employee, journey for a full view of the service experience.

Ethnographic data is ideal input for mapping the customer experience journey, as it illuminates the particulars of the experience – the steps, phases, touchpoints, pain points, moments of delight, emotional experience – as well as the broader context beyond the moment when the product or service overlaps with the customer's life.

Ecosystem and journey mapping, based on ethnographic data of what people do, say, and feel, reveals the total experience as more than merely the sum of individual processes strung together across departments. Customers, as they traverse touchpoints across the lifecycle of their engagement, formulate their opinions of the overall experience and the meaning that the product or service carries in their lives. Understanding meaning rarely occurs from looking at individual interactions, but rather by looking at the wider context of what someone needs or wants.

Being customer-centric invites and necessitates multifunctional conversations. Since the customer's experience inevitably traverses organizational silos and functional area boundaries, ethnographic research initiatives tend to catalyze cross-group collaboration. Researchers will be required to develop organizational change and facilitation skills that encourage stakeholder participation, buy-in, sense making and action taking.

In 2011, I led an ethnographic study to understand how new customers interacted with the bank through all the available channels (branch, ATM, phone, online, etc.), and, for many of these group stakeholders, it was the first time they had really talked to one another (for the complete case study see: Beers, Stinson, & Yeager, 2011). The study became the platform for opening up silos and bringing people together who had little occasion to collaborate previously. The opportunity to see the multichannel experience from the customer's point of view sparked new thinking and conversations which eventually led to tangible actions to improve the customer experience. The more complete view of the bank's touchpoint ecosystem encouraged cross-channel collaboration and led to new initiatives, including redesigning the new-customer onboarding program to address customer pain points and provide more support during "moments of truth," such as funding a new account or activating a new ATM card.

Just as companies don't often have a clear picture of their customers' behavior and motivation, they often have many blind spots regarding their own processes and how these fit together over the customer engagement lifecycle. Ethnographic research that matches behind-the-scenes activities with experience outcomes can illuminate the fragmentation and unintended poor experience that can ensue from siloed organizational structures and activities. For instance, we learned that new customers saw the branch as "ground zero" for getting all their questions answered, but bankers were often left looking for answers themselves when the question involved another channel, such as Bill Pay in online banking. Bankers needed easier ways to connect with channel experts to obtain accurate information without being subjected to even more formal training. A channel hotline allowed bankers to quickly reach online experts who could explain the intricacies of a service. This allowed the banker to get help while maintaining face in front of the customer and reduced both hand-offs and the tendency for bankers to unintentionally pass along inaccurate information when they were not entirely sure of their answer.

Organizational learning and change occurs as the business reconciles its own internally held assumptions – embedded in its strategies, processes, and structure – with how customers experience the results across the lifecycle of engagement. What does it all add up to? What's in and out of alignment with intentions? Where are the points of friction in the system? The organizational change implications are potentially massive when companies start to understand their customer's experience and their own processes holistically.

Creating shared understanding

Good experiences happen at the intersection of customer needs, business goals, technology enablers, and the people that bring it all to fruition. It is a participatory process that requires teams of people to negotiate and reconcile all these elements across the ecosystem. It is at this intersection that positive customer experiences that produce business value can be attained. But all these viewpoints and factors must be discussed, understood, and reconciled "through dialogue in a human community" for true collaboration to occur (Boland, 1987, p. 377).

Researchers in corporations always represent just one discipline on a larger, multifunctional team. In an organization focused on creating digital experiences, such as the one that I work in, typical functions include product and project managers, business analysts, user-experience designers, researchers, behavioral analytics analysts, content strategists, front-end developers, back-end database engineers, and technical architects. These teams are brought together to execute simple solutions for customers amidst tremendous complexity. We must combine our functional expertise, understand how we each contribute to the solution, and collectively ensure we are solving the right problems. Up-front time and attention must be devoted to alignment activities that result in shared understanding of what we are trying to achieve and why.

When all these different functions come together on a new project, the first job is to collectively understand the system – the current state of the product or service – the stakeholders involved on the project and their points of view, and what opportunities exist. Ambiguity abounds at this stage as team members are meeting, perhaps for the first time, roles and responsibilities are being established, and scope and timelines need to be defined.

In typical business-led projects, scope is largely driven by timelines and costs, even when user needs and pain points are included in the mix. But, unless the multidisciplinary project team's early conversations are designed to include user needs, the scope-definition phase can feel less like collaboration and more like the business functions handing off orders to the design team.

Let me illustrate with an example. Recently, a multifunctional team came together to redesign a complex commercial banking application. Business came to the table with a wish list of functional requirements they hoped to

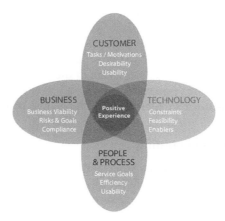

Figure 2.2 Good experiences are created by aligning strategies, technologies, and processes with customer expectations.

include in this project. This information was transferred into a draft of an official deliverable called a *project scope document*. The designers came to the project kick-off with their own questions based on years of working on this application but found little opening to dialogue and "open up" the items in the scope document, discuss what they meant, and how their implementation might improve the application.

Business and Design had the same goal – to reduce ambiguity and move the project forward – but different criteria and means for getting there. Business wanted to quickly lock in scope to obtain project funding and drive toward execution. But Design needed to more fully understand the terminology, opportunities, implications, and trade-offs being made before committing to scope. The team dynamic quickly became tense. Business felt Design was slowing down the project scope-approval process by unnecessarily getting into more detail than was necessary at the start of the project. Design felt that we must "go slow to go fast" to achieve shared understanding and create alignment about the problems to solve and how to solve them.

Just as good end-user experiences cannot be created without multifunctional collaboration, coming to a shared understanding cannot happen without dialogue. Dialogue, like collaboration, equals more than the sum of its parts; it enables people to translate terminology for one another and develop alignment around a common purpose, which are critical precursors to coordinated action. Dialogue involves group interpreting and translating processes during which reconciliation between diverse perspectives and alignment can occur (Weick & Van Orden, 1990). These activities are particularly important at the beginning of a project.

These conversations do not happen automatically; they have to be intentionally designed into the project's agenda. Herbert Simon, in *The Sciences of the Artificial* (1969, p. 55), defines *design* as the "transformation of existing conditions into preferred ones," and, in this case, what needed transformation was not just the software application but also the "us/them" dynamic between Design and Business. Design convinced the product manager to try something new – use design-thinking visualization techniques to facilitate alignment, and, in so doing, transform scope definition from a business-led activity to one that was truly collaborative.

Researchers partnered with Design and Business to synthesize previous research. We also spent time pulling apart the draft scope document, which was packed with technical and business terminology that was ambiguous and unevenly understood across the multifunctional team. As the functions and features were isolated, we also attempted to translate the language into customer needs. Designers then further transformed this information by creating "opportunity cards" – simple visualizations of each proposed feature – for instance, "customize reports" or "personalization" – and used these cards to facilitate a whole-team discussion of what these terms actually meant, how important the team thought they were, and how difficult they would be to execute. A digital version was offered to remote participants who could track what was going on in the meeting room through conferencing software.

Being visual instead of explanatory allowed the multifunctional team to discuss the opportunities freely and focus on the intended end-user experience first before codifying them in the official project scope document. Facilitators presented the opportunity cards as individual cut-outs so they could be moved around and used, hands on, by the team in our in-person working session. They were not fixed, or final; they could be edited. They even had blanks for new and unforeseen opportunities.

After we gained group clarity on the proposed opportunity, we plotted the card along the x-axis to prioritize importance relative to the other opportunities. Next, the facilitators drew the y-axis and the group prioritized again according to our collective sense of how difficult the opportunity would be to implement. We were calibrating user and business goals with organizational processes and technological capabilities through real-time, participatory dialogue.

The process and the outputs of this session were extraordinary; we went from polarized discussions between Business and Design to a multifunctional

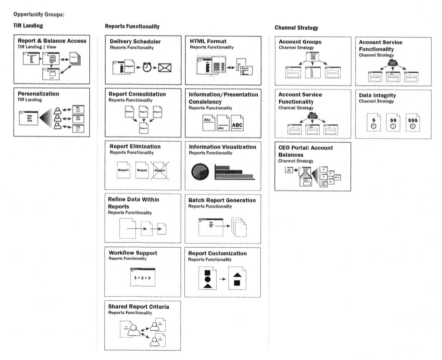

Figure 2.3 Opportunity cards were created by "pulling apart" the scope document and translating the feature and function terminology into language that described the customer's needs.

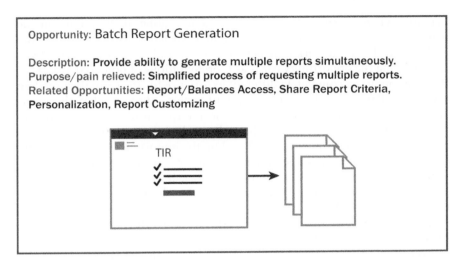

Opportunity: Batch Report Generation

Description: **Provide ability to generate multiple reports simultaneously.**
Purpose/pain relieved: **Simplified process of requesting multiple reports.**
Related Opportunities: **Report/Balances Access, Share Report Criteria,**
Personalization, Report Customizing

TIR

Figure 2.4 Opportunity card detail for batch report generation: each opportunity card has a simple graphic representation, symbolic of the opportunity, and a very short description of the function, with a purpose statement and some related opportunities.

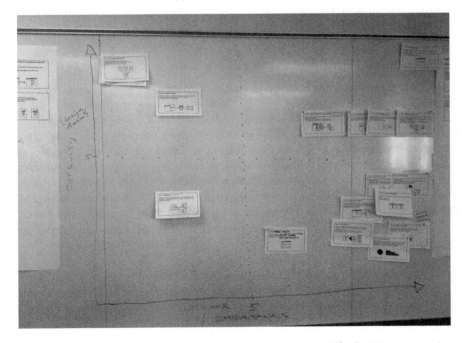

Figure 2.5 Importance/Difficulty Matrix (The Importance/Difficulty Matrix exercise was taught to us in the context of human-centered facilitation training taught by the LUMA Institute. More about LUMA can be found on their website: www.luma-institute.com)

dialogue where a true, shared understanding among all functions on the team was achieved. The facilitation invited participatory problem solving and provided a framework in which decisions could be made efficiently as a group. Using the opportunity cards as representations of potential aspects of the solution was a completely different experience for the team then reading through a flat scope document. We had time to discuss what the terms actually meant and to reconcile diverse interpretations. The visual and modular nature of the exercise further enhanced the discussion as participants could see how opportunity cards placed on the importance/difficulty matrix played off one another, something that would not have occurred if we dealt with each item in linear isolation. This workshop also led us to identify hypotheses for early Discovery user research. The team came out of the one-day session with a clear, shared understanding of what the terms meant, their relative priority based on importance and difficulty, and a list of hypotheses to explore with users.

Even though this was more of a design-led, rather than a research-led, workshop, the tight collaboration between Design and Research contributed to the positive outcome by grounding the opportunities in previous research findings and taking the hypotheses as a next step to be carried out by Research. In this example, combining a holistic mindset with an emphasis on dialogue to achieve shared understanding resulted in team alignment and commitment to shared objectives and next steps.

Design-oriented problem solving

The shift of power from business to people signals a need for organizations – and the teams of employees within them – to transform how they work together and produce value. User-centered design (UCD) is a proven approach and set of methods that can support organizations on their path to become more customer-centric (Beers & Whitney, 2006). UCD is a product-development process that involves learning from and incorporating end-user feedback throughout the entire product lifecycle, giving researchers a large role to play. For product- or technology-centric organizations, user-centered design methodology can represent a radical shift in mindset and work practices. Essentially, UCD puts people and their needs, goals, and tasks on par with the organization's business goals and technology capabilities:

> The chief difference from other product design philosophies is that user-centered design tries to optimize the product around how users can, want, or need to use the product, rather than forcing the users to change their behavior to accommodate the product.
>
> (http://en.wikipedia.org/wiki/User-centered_design)

The rise of UCD practices in business acknowledges that products and services need to work well for the people who use them.

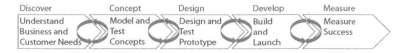

Figure 2.6 User-centered design process.

In today's experience-driven economy, UCD helps to mitigate risk of an unsuccessful product by getting the noise out of the system earlier. Research contributes to this goal by going directly to users to observe and gather feedback using in-process prototypes and helping the team learn so it can iterate the design of the product toward an optimal solution. Figure 2.6 shows our generic UCD process model at Wells Fargo.

The circular arrows represent iteration based on learning from feedback. The iterative nature means that UCD is inherently an organizational learning process. Learning occurs when "out there" insights gathered by Research are brought in as points of comparison with internally held organizational assumptions. Comparing people's "out there" expectations and experiences to "in here" organizational assumptions strikes at the heart of what is most valuable about customer research. Ethnographic insight is most powerful in helping organizations learn and innovate when the "what" of people's lived experience is combined and calibrated with the "how" of meeting business goals. When this comparative aspect is orchestrated intentionally it has the power to transform organizations.

Cycles of iteration through learning and reconciling "out there" perceptions with "in here" assumptions are supported by the concept of divergence and convergence, which is intrinsic to the UCD process.

The divergent and convergent double-diamond diagram is likely familiar to ethnographic researchers and designers practicing UCD. It begins with a point of focus, such as an area of inquiry, but then diverges as the data, and the complexity of making sense of that data, floods in. The analysis process leads us back out of ambiguity toward honing in on understanding context, the critical elements of experience, and potential problems to solve. Kerry Bodine, from Forrester Research, writes:

> Designers often describe the end-to-end design process as a double diamond. It starts at a singular point – the initial focus for the project – but quickly diverges as the research uncovers new insights and potential problems to solve. The process converges to the midpoint as teams synthesize the research findings and reframe the project focus. The process diverges again as teams brainstorm a broad range of possible solutions and start to prototype. Lastly, refinement through multiple rounds of prototyping and testing converges the process to its final point: the design solution.
>
> (Bodine, 2012)

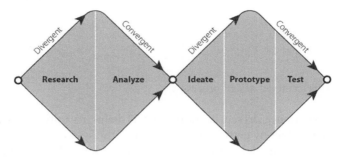

Figure 2.7 User-centered design involves convergent and divergent activities (Diagram from Bodine, 2012).

A story illustrates the power of juxtaposition and comparison along with the activities of divergence and convergence to ensure that teams are aware of the ecosystem dynamics at play.

Years ago, at a consulting firm where I held the title "Experience Modeler," a team set out to redesign the website of a non-profit foundation offering resources for parents whose children experienced learning disabilities. Following a UCD process, the team sent researchers to conduct ethnography – a divergent activity that casts the inquiry net wide – with mothers of kids with learning disabilities. The rich insights offered portraits of moms who worked tirelessly to get their kids the medical, therapeutic, and educational resources that they needed; they were true advocates and warriors on behalf of their children, accustomed to encountering obstacles and refusing to take "no" for an answer.

The insights into the moms' experiences were successful in providing designers with empathy and context from which to redesign the site. But researchers had cast the net wider than just the moms and had also conducted stakeholder interviews with the foundation's staff. They noticed that the staff often spoke about these mothers in negative terms, such as referring to them as "rabid" or "combative." Researchers brought both sets of data to a sense-making, analysis workshop. The leadership was shaken by the dissonance between the foundation's mission and the staff's attitudes toward the mothers they served. By taking a broad, holistic perspective and casting the inquiry net wide – diverging – the project team was able to converge on the decision to work on resolving the negative conception of its target audience and improving the foundation's internal culture before moving forward with the redesign. This example also illustrates the point that insights can catalyze organizational change that then thrusts researchers into the dual role of change agent.

Another type of convergence/divergence activity involves synthesizing the massive amount of data that comes out of ethnographic research into visual representations called experience models. This is where academically trained researchers must expand their capabilities, and, sometimes, enlist the help of their design colleagues. Experience Models visually crystallize the current state and suggest opportunities for better meeting people's needs – they often act like headlights for the product teams that use them.

These models communicate the patterns of how people organize their experience and represent the culmination of rigorous data analysis. Experience models are typically arrived at and agreed upon collaboratively, building veracity into the analysis process and buy-in for the findings and recommendations. Experience models that ring true within the organization and thus live on, can be said to attain experiential significance:

> Experiential significance is a transformative analogue to statistical significance. It is felt through rigorous, collaborative analysis when an emerging model is both easily grasped by organizational stakeholders and resonates with data-driven truths and intuitive "rightness." Models such as these are mental tools that can provide a "Eureka!" spark for new thinking.
>
> (Cayla, Beers, & Arnould, 2014, p. 58)

These models also provide a container for the ethnographic insights to live on, providing shorthand for teams to refer to and use the learning for years to come.

By example, the simple model shown in Figure 2.8 was dubbed the "View/ Do" loop within Wells Fargo and communicated our key findings that when people are doing their routine financial tasks they are largely on automatic pilot and do not often switch into "learning" or "discovery" mode when it comes to exploring online banking.

This experience model showed highlighted that information and functionality available on the site was not discovered within the user's routines and it helped crystallize the problem we were trying to solve within a redesign – undiscovered and, thus underutilized, functionality that lived outside this loop – and it became shorthand for pursuing a strategy of in-context content and features. In fact, the project team tasked with

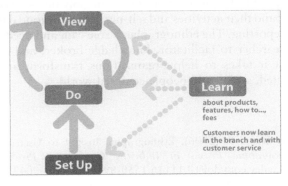

Figure 2.8 Experience models are thinking tools.

redesign embraced the model so wholeheartedly that they 'riffed' off the model's View/Do label and named the overall project VooDoo.

For models to attain experiential significance, or act as an "experiential guidepost," they must be easy to grasp and have resonance within the organization (Blomberg, Burrel, & Guest, 2009). Models represent a point of convergence in the ethnographic process, distilling data and findings into "boundary objects" that team members can point to, discuss, and use to arrive at shared understanding (Star & Griesemer, 1989). In my work, I have repeatedly seen that a visual representation – such as an experience model or the opportunity cards discussed earlier – do a superior job of generating discussion and agreement, as opposed to discussion alone or narrative, non-visual documents.

Conclusion

> *If we are going to create organizations that can thrive in today's more social world … we don't need our organizations to be better machines. We need our organizations to be more human.*
>
> (Notter & Grant, 2011, p. 95)

In complex, large organizations, multifunctional project teams are the rule. Every function – be it engineering, product management, design, marketing – comes in with particular expertise and focus. This expertise and focus acts like a lens that colors how the team members perceive and understand the issues and problems they have come together to solve. Activities dedicated to understanding the ecosystem, translating viewpoints, and learning through experimentation and iteration are critical to team alignment, and, ultimately, successful execution.

Researchers have unique perspectives, skills, and a critical role that they can occupy to help organizations become more human. The capabilities described in this chapter – embracing a holistic mindset, creating shared understanding, and design-oriented problem solving – necessitate that researchers expand their activities and self-perception beyond data collection, analysis, and reporting. The ethnographer's role can, and needs to, progress from mere researcher to facilitator, knowledge broker, and change agent. We have what it takes to help organizations transform and succeed in today's connected, social, and people-centered world.

References

Beers, R., & Whitney, P. (2006). Ethnographic Insight to User-centered Design Tools. *Ethnographic Praxis in Industry Conference Proceedings.* http://onlinelibrary.wiley.com/doi/10.1111/j.1559-8918.2006.tb00043.x/pdf

Beers, R., Stinson, T. & Yeager, J. (2011). Ethnography as a Catalyst for Organizational Change: Creating a Multichannel Customer Experience.

Ethnographic Praxis in Industry Conference Proceedings. http://epiconference. com/2012/sites/epiconference.com.2012/files/attachments/article/add/EPIC2012-Proceedings.pdf

Blomberg, J., Burrel, M., & Guest, G. (2009). An ethnographic approach to design. In A. Sears & J. A. Jacko (Eds.), *Human-Computer Interaction: Development process* (Google eBook). CRC Press, 964–987.

Bodine, K. (2011. Updated, 2013). The Customer Experience Ecosystem. *Forrester Research.* www.forrester.com/The+Customer+Experience+Ecosystem/fulltext/-/ E-RES59115

Bodine, K. (2012). Q&A: Customer Experience Design. June 22, 2012. *Forrester Research.* www.forrester.com/Executive+QA+Customer+Experience+Design/ fulltext/-/E-RES75961

Boland, R. J. (1987). The in-formation of information systems. In R. J. Boland & R. A. Hirschheim (Eds.), *Critical Issues in Information Systems Research.* New York: Wiley, 363–394.

Boland, R. J., Tenkasi, R. V., & Te'eni, D. (1994). Designing information technology to support distributed cognition. *Organization Science*, 5(3), 456–475.

Brown, J. S., & Duguid, P. (1991). Organizational learning and communities-of-practice: Toward a unified view of working, learning, and innovation. *Organization Science*, 2, 40–57.

Cayla, J., Beers, R., & Arnould, E. (Winter 2014). Stories that deliver business insights. *MIT Sloan Management Review*, 55(2), 55–62.

Cooperstein, D. (2013). Competitive Strategy in the Age of the Customer: Only Customer-Obsessed Enterprises Can Survive Disruption. *Forrester Research.* www.forrester.com/Competitive+Strategy+In+The+Age+Of+The+Customer/ fulltext/-/ERES59159.

Easterby-Smith, M., Snell, R., & Gherardi, S. (1998). Organizational learning and learning organization: Diverging communities of practice? *Management Learning*, 29, 259–272.

Merchant, N. (2012). *11 Rules for Creating Value in the Social Era.* Cambridge, MA: Harvard Business Press Books.

Neumeier, M. (August 13, 2008). Designing the Future of Business. *Business Week.* www.businessweek.com/stories/2008-08-13/designing-the-future-of-business businessweekbusiness-news-stock-market-and-financial-advice

Notter, J., & Grant, M. (2011). *Humanize: How people-centric organizations succeed in a social world.* Indianapolis, IN: Que Press.

Senge, P. M. (1990). *The Fifth Discipline: The art of the learning organization.* New York: Doubleday.

Simon, H. A. (1969). *The Sciences of the Artificial.* Cambridge, MA: MIT Press.

Star, S. L., & Griesemer, J. R. (1989). Institutional ecology, 'translations' and boundary objects: Amateurs and professionals. *Berkeley's Museum of Vertebrate Zoology. Social Studies of Science*, 19, 387–420.

Weick, K., & Van Orden, P. (1990). Organizing on a global scale. In N. Tichy, (Ed.), *Human Resource Management*, 29, 49–62.

3 Success despite the silos

System-wide innovation and collaboration

Elizabeth K. Briody and Ken C. Erickson

Introduction

People who work in large organizations often lament the decentralized structures that define their work functions and day-to-day activities. Finance, IT, supply chain, legal, and any number of other organizational functions exhibit cultures that are distinctive in their work practices, processes, and perspectives. Colloquially referred to as *silos*, these internal organizational units are often characterized as impenetrable, and are frequently the subject of finger pointing and blame. They seem to stand in opposition to each other; the people within them seem to be optimizing for their own individual area rather than for the wellbeing of the wider corporate whole.

Yet, collaboration is typically expected across silos since multiple functional areas must contribute to getting the work of the organization done. We define *collaboration* as "working in concert with others in the pursuit of particular goals" (Briody, Trotter, and Meerwarth 2010, p. 7). Moreover, system- or organization-wide innovation is often necessary to enable organizations to respond to environmental pressures and market challenges, improve their products and services over time, and address internal organizational issues. We use Rogers' (2003, p. 12) definition of *innovation*: "an idea, practice, or object that is perceived as new by an individual or other unit of adoption." We focus primarily on ethnographic contexts in which we saw innovation attempted. For us, system-wide innovation implies penetration of the innovation across the entire system such that the organizational structure and dynamics support the innovation. Given the tendency to align *within silos* as part of an organizational function, and the overarching organizational goal to develop and deliver products and services (sometimes requiring innovation) *across silos*, organizational members typically find themselves embroiled in internal contradictions and conflict. We argue that understanding the interplay between silo-ed organizational structure and collaboration offers clues to innovation success. Indeed, the presence of specific organizational-culture characteristics, including collaboration, is responsible for the realization of system-wide innovation.

Literature focus

Scholars have used the term *silo* to refer to the "horizontal axis" or areas of specialization within a hierarchical organization (Diamond, Stein, and Allcorn 2002, p. 280). Such divisions are characterized by a single function, product, or area of focus just as cylindrical storage containers on farms are used for storing a single type of food for livestock (Vermeulen, Puranam, and Gulati 2010, p. 72; Neebe 1987, p. 815). Applying this farm metaphor to business organizations enables understanding of how large organizations are structured and differentiated based on areas of expertise, training, and day-to-day work activities. Indeed, organizations purposely cluster specialized knowledge and competencies together to gain depth as well as economies of scale (Gulati 2007, p. 2). Silos create "efficient structures for executing strategy" (Kleinbaum, Stuart, and Tushman 2008, p. 1). Moreover, the boundaries between silos can be both "productive and anxiety reducing" since the "purpose, responsibility, and authority and coordination of work" within them are well defined (Diamond, Stein, and Allcorn 2002, p. 293).

Silos as a metaphor for dysfunction

Yet, the silo metaphor is typically employed to signal difficulties in organizational functioning. For instance, Lencioni (2006) points out that

> Silos are nothing more than the barriers that exist between departments within an organization, causing people who are supposed to be on the same team to work against one another. And whether we call this phenomenon departmental politics, divisional rivalry, or turf warfare, it is one of the most frustrating aspects of life in any sizeable organization.
> (p. 175)

Similarly, Diamond, Allcorn, and Stein (2004, p. 46) indicate that an "'us versus them' mindset" and "inter-silo cultural chauvinism" appear in the internal, everyday discourse about other parts of the organization. The term *silo* has been used to describe organizations and their management teams "that lack the desire or motivation to coordinate (at worst, even communicate) with other entities in the same organization.... High costs are borne from duplication of effort, inconsistencies, and inefficiencies" (Serrat 2010, pp. 1–2). As an example, Intensive Care Units have been portrayed as a "parallel, but minimally interactive work environment" since both physicians and nurses "interact only briefly during rounds and at the bedside of unstable patients" (Curtis and Shannon 2006, p. 16). Cilliers and Greyvenstein (2012, pp. 3–4) summarize much of the literature, emphasizing both the "silo as invisible barrier" and the "silo as container," and conclude (2012, p. 8) that the "silo mentality" is tied to "destructive differentiation and breaking down of connection."

Collaboration as goal and remedy

The scholarly literature on silos, which spans business types ranging from manufacturing (Aaker 2013) through public administration (Bundred 2006), points to many tactical remedies to the problems that arise from organizational silos. These prescriptions include structural changes to the organization (Cash, Earl, and Morison 2008; Vermeulen, Puranam, and Gulati 2010), spatial rearrangements to encourage interaction (Thomas and Hern 2006), and reorganized IT efforts (Bannister 2001), among others. All these solutions aim for the same result. They point to a general consensus in the literature that collaboration and communication are both the process for and the solution to the issues experienced by silo-ed organizations. "In most situations, silos rise up not because of what executives are doing purposefully but rather because of what they are failing to do: provide themselves and their employees with a compelling context for working together" (Lencioni 2006, p. 175). Collaboration and cooperation are said to become "trapped" within the silos, whether those units are based on function, product, geography, or market (Vermeulen, Puranam, and Gulati 2010, p. 72). Therefore, Vermeulen and colleagues propose an organizational shake-up based on the results of a "corporate cholesterol test" or questionnaire to corporate managers. If employee interaction is limited largely to within-group contact, communication breakdowns occur along silo boundaries, well-established routines are not questioned, and influential groups and individuals command most of the firm's resources, then some cross-silo restructuring is needed.

Strategies to foster collaboration

Researchers from a wide array of disciplines (e.g., health care, business, human-computer interaction, library science) have proposed ways to improve organizational functioning in silo-ed structures through collaborative approaches. Interprofessional education is one step in raising awareness of the broader work context, and in acquainting young professionals with team-based approaches to work (Bandali *et al.* 2011; Miller *et al.*, 2010; Margarlit *et al.* 2009; Herbert 2005). Shirey (2006) argues that "intrapreneurs" or organizational change agents such as clinical nurse specialists can help break down professional silos. However, others suggest that the interdisciplinary activity is "far too low" in numbers (Newhouse and Spring 2010, p. 312) – particularly within academic and clinical settings – and that a paradigm shift needs to occur in which groups rather than individuals are rewarded. In business organizations defined by sharply silo-ed structures, collaboration is not rewarded – whether internally among employees of different silos, or externally with customers, suppliers, and partners (Gulati 2007). Incentives are an important catalyst for collaboration to thrive as reported in endeavors involving libraries, archives, and museums, though other catalysts may be necessary as well including a vision, a mandate, resources, and trust (Zorich *et al.* 2008), or direct involvement in the initiative such as from a user community (Foster 2013).

Collaboration, organizational innovation, and transformation

Many scholars have outlined processes or frameworks for encouraging collaboration, and through that collaboration, the successful implementation of organizational innovations or change. Discussing American organizations in general, Diamond, Stein, and Allcorn (2002, pp. 294–295) suggest involving both management and employees in a "shared process" of planning and implementing organizational change. Organizational learning and problem solving become the focal points, rather than the "defensive routines of the silo mentality" (2002, p. 286). Lencioni (2006) offers a four-part model for addressing silo problems and achieving organizational goals:

1 Developing a thematic goal, a top priority, that is time limited (i.e., between 6–12 months) and shared by the entire organization (e.g., rebuild our credibility in the market)
2 Defining objectives that are the building blocks of the thematic goal (e.g., establish a comprehensive strategy, create a unified marketing message)
3 Including standard operating objectives – the ongoing organizational priorities (e.g., market share by product category, customer satisfaction)
4 Metrics or ways with which to measure progress

Simplifying and measuring the organization's work in this way breaks down the silos and aligns organizational members toward the future. In perhaps one of the most well-known silo-ed corporations in the world, Briody, Trotter, and Meerwarth (2010) document the decentralized structure and autonomous culture of General Motors (GM) and propose models to create an ideal culture based on collaboration and processes, and tools to achieve that ideal.

Less well depicted in the literature is whether, and under what conditions, collaboration emerges in the process of innovating in a silo-ed organizational structure. In the event that collaboration takes hold, it does so within a broader, dynamic cultural context. Neither the desire to collaborate (Briody, Trotter, and Meerwarth 2010), nor the prescription to collaborate (cf., Lencioni 2006) offer insights into what actually happens when collaboration is attempted. Important insights about silo bridging are beginning to emerge from quantitative social network analysis of electronic communication in organizations. Recent work there reports that "although theories of communication and coordination are central ... we have theories and assumptions but little empirical evidence about the structure of communication in the modern, complex organization" (Kleinbaum, Stuart, and Tushman 2008, p. 45). Thus, there is little descriptive, in-context detail on the day-to-day culture of the silos in relation to other silos or the sequence of actions as the innovation progresses through the organization.

The same might be said of much of the research on innovation in business, which often uses large-scale, experience-distant data sets to explore hypotheses about the effects of cross-company collaboration, the effects of industrial clustering, or the effects of organizational culture on innovation. Such studies often depict innovation as the dependent variable that is operationalized using measures such as patent applications or manager responses to surveys about innovation. On the one hand, reductive proxy measures are useful for comparative work and hypothesis testing. On the other hand, they oversimplify the many ways in which innovation, however defined, actually happens in organizational practice. From an anthropological point of view, the notion of innovation seems under-theorized. Ethnographers' concern with "counting to one" (Kirk and Miller 1986, p. 9), that is, identifying which characteristics or influencers contribute to any given issue, has not yet been clearly addressed:

> Only rarely have observation methodologies been employed which would enable researchers to access the activity level theories-in-use enacted in the workplace. Yet, it is at this 'micro level' that the managerial reality enfolds every day, therefore a theory of innovation needs to connect the action (*praxis*) with the managerial and academic theories (*practice*) by understanding the role of agents (*practitioners*).
> (Crossan and Apaydin 2010, pp. 1178–1179).

In this chapter, we present examples of organizational practice and praxis in three organizations in which formally designated and informally driven leaders recognize the importance of external environmental changes, respond to them with organizational process or product innovations, and experience varying degrees of innovation success. In the examples involving an intimate apparel company, only halting efforts at cross-silo collaboration were evident. In the GM example involving one of its first global vehicle programs, there was an attempt at mandated cross-silo collaboration but without changing any of the relevant structural mechanisms to support it. In the examples associated with a large hospital, cross-silo collaboration was sometimes helpful for innovation success and sometimes not. We focus our attention on the following questions:

- What accounts for these different organizational experiences related to system-wide innovation?
- What role does collaboration play in system-wide innovation?
- What cultural responses are activated within and across silos during innovation?

Studies of innovation as process are "underdeveloped in the literature" (Crossan and Apaydin 2010, p. 1167). The ethnographic vantage point we offer is not only a step toward crafting ethnographic accounts of innovation in the everyday context of organizational culture, but also addresses the problem of silos. We believe this approach is a useful, relevant, and timely contribution to innovation research as well as to those organizational leaders trying to innovate.

Data and methods

Three different ethnographic research projects on which we worked either individually or as members of larger research teams form the basis of our analysis. The projects were unrelated to each other and had their own research goals. We brought the three projects together to write this chapter. Articles and chapters have been published about aspects of the global vehicle program (Briody 2010, 2013; Ferraro and Briody 2013; Briody, Cavusgil, and Miller 2004), but not yet about the other two organizations.

Intimate apparel firm

Our mixed-methods approach was designed to examine the robustness of links in the value chain (i.e., design to marketing to retail to shoppers and end users), assess the effects of organizational history and culture on sales, and explore the relationship between customer preferences and practices on corporate strategy. We conducted 22 interviews with managerial and higher-ranking executives (lasting 1 hour on average), nine interviews with managers of company-owned outlet stores, and informal discussions with store clerks and store managers at retail locations around the U.S. We gathered data from 26 in-home interviews and home tours (lasting 90 minutes on average) with women in seven U.S. cities, and two free-listing exercises with 10 of these women, to document the cultural categories through which women understood intimate wear. We also conducted in-store participant observation with shoppers to understand how women understood and valued the intimate wear they encountered – to understand what Desjeux and Zheng (2002) refer to as the *product itinerary*, that is, the purchase and use of the product understood in context. These methods, along with exploration of the firm's website and its competitors' websites, helped us understand how and where corporate and consumer views differed.

Because five researchers were involved due to the geographical spread of the project (including Erickson and Briody), we used a daily blog to communicate and discuss our initial thoughts and experiences. We shared our blog with our in-company partners. Two of us took the lead in analyzing the ethnographic material. We used content analysis to identify salient themes and patterns from the interviews and observations, comparing them with the blog discussions, and validating them with the views and experiences of other researchers and with our in-company partners.

Global vehicle program

This project, carried out by a sole in-house researcher (Briody), was designed to explore the overall effectiveness of a GM global vehicle program in its engineering phase. Ninety-one employees working at one U.S. location participated in interviews that lasted 1 hour on average. The interviews focused on the program's activities and issues, as well as on ideas for improving program performance. To gain an understanding of the ways technical and organizational-culture issues were negotiated, observations of 23 of the program's engineering and business meetings occurred; these meetings took place in large conference rooms and lasted 3.5 hours on average. Program documents were also collected. Finally, 26 presentations were given to members of the global program as well as the senior leadership across the corporation to validate and expand upon the findings and recommendations.

This research design allowed the comparison of interview data with both observations at meetings and program documents. The analysis was intended to be inductive and iterative due to the organizational and technical complexity of the global program. Content analysis was the key analytic technique used to capture cultural themes. Validation occurred both through one-on-one discussions and large-scale presentations.

Hospital

Seven researchers (including Briody and six hospital employees) used a variety of ethnographic methods in their project to improve patient hospital experiences. The data collection included 101 interviews with hospital staff and leadership, 51 meetings involving hospital personnel, and 46 observations on nursing floors, in diagnostic areas, and in waiting rooms. On average, the interviews lasted about 45 minutes, the meetings about 80 minutes, and the observations about 75 minutes. Our focus was on understanding the current state and eliciting the ideal state of the patient experience, as well as figuring out what aspects of the patient experience were working well, and those necessitating improvement. The project scope did not include direct interactions with patients *per se* because the project sponsors believed they already understood the patient experience from earlier projects; instead, they wanted to learn about the patient experience based on staff observations and perspectives. However, some of our interviews were with hospital employees who had been hospitalized or whose family members had been hospitalized.

We used three techniques to analyze the hospital data: content analysis of the qualitative data, discourse analysis of tape-recorded hospital meetings, and statistical analysis of key variables. We validated our findings through the use of different methods, data sources, and members of our research team. For example, we were able to compare our ethnographic results with the findings compiled from patient focus groups conducted 2 years earlier.

Background

Rationale for organizational comparison

All three organizations have headquarters in the U.S. As such, they share certain structural and relationship-based attributes. First, each organization is embedded within a layered corporate hierarchy in which sharp distinctions exist between the senior leadership team and all other employees. For example, an employee from the intimate apparel firm stated, "The fifth floor (which houses the senior leadership team) says that they look across for opportunities for people. But someone has to represent and sponsor you." Second, status, authority, and power matter enormously within the various functions and divisions associated with the three corporate hierarchies. Third, salary and career path are tied to these functional and divisional silos, with little cross-silo job rotation. The end result is that employee allegiance and daily social interaction is primarily focused within one's own silo. These structural and behavioral features were confirmed in the expressions employees used to describe their place of work and the jobs they performed. We routinely heard phrases and terms such as *turf wars*, *fiefdom*, *tribe*, *territory*, and *handoff* in all three organizations.

Marketplace challenges

Employees associated with each case recognized that the external environment surrounding their organization was in flux and having a direct effect on their organization's performance. They were able to articulate specific pressures that heightened concerns about their organization's long-term competitiveness regionally (hospital), nationally (intimate apparel), and globally (vehicle program). Employees pointed to the necessity of innovation – whether in organizational processes or products/services or both, while complaining about the difficulty of shaping a coordinated response to emerging external pressures. Additionally, they specified the importance of the customer perspective, recognizing that favorable customer evaluations of products/services lead to return customers and enhanced image in the marketplace.

A corporate strategy to compete in retail

Revenue from the intimate apparel manufacturer had been flat for several years prior to the study, except in 2008–09 when it took a deep dive due to the recession. Part of the company's mission at that time was to "sell more, spend less, (and) generate cash." There had been several rounds of layoffs to cut costs. Executives and brand-managers in this global, U.S.-based apparel firm sought to understand women's changing needs for intimate apparel (e.g., younger women wanted bras earlier in their lives, obesity had been on the rise since the 1960s [National Institutes of Health, 2012]). A key competitor firm, Victoria's Secret, had emerged as a market leader, pressuring the company to re-examine its positioning, retail approaches, and product offerings. A decision was made to produce women's bras and panties that were largely white, beige, or black, and which would be sold primarily through the company's key retail outlets: big-box retailers like Walmart and Target, and mid-tier retailers like Kohl's and Marshalls.

An experiment in global engineering

The establishment of global vehicle programs at GM resulted in part from a desire to achieve global economies of scale in product development, thereby reducing costs and improving profitability, quality, and lead time. An initial attempt to launch a global program had failed. However, senior management believed that a single vehicle underbody could be developed to serve as the platform for numerous car models; these models could then be adapted for different geographies, terrains, and regulatory requirements. As such, global programs were experimental. Senior leaders assembled three engineering units associated with multiple markets worldwide to do the program's development work. In this early engineering phase, key program personnel were located in or re-located to the U.S.

A decision to improve the patient experience

Changes in U.S. health care policy have affected the view of the physician-patient relationship and the delivery of patient care. In response to the passage of the Affordable Health Care Act, and despite the uncertainties surrounding it, the hospital began a concerted effort to plan for changes in reimbursement rates, install and train staff on various forms of health IT, and put in place strategies to cope with shortages of primary care physicians. Of immediate concern was the loss of millions of Medicare dollars if patient satisfaction scores did not improve significantly. The hospital administration set aside resources to try to create and sustain a patient-centric hospital culture.

Model of System-wide innovation

We present our model of system-wide innovation success to orient and guide the ethnographic descriptions of our three silo-ed organizations. The model consists of five organizational-culture features (see Figure 3.1). First, collaboration is an essential part of the model. Without organizational

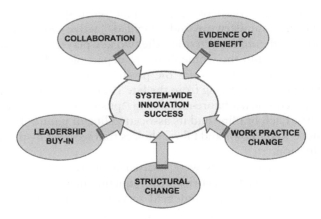

Figure 3.1 Features tied to system-wide innovation success. (Image courtesy of Elizabeth Briody.)

members working cooperatively and across organizational units (or silos) together, the innovation would not be sustained. Second, leadership buy-in – support for and advocacy of the innovation – matters for system-wide innovation. Third, structural change in the organization's functioning occurs. Such changes might include reporting relationships, roles, networks, use of incentives, and organizational rules. Fourth, work practice change, such as what work tasks are done and how these tasks are done, contributes to successful system-wide innovation. Finally, the model incorporates a feature we term *evidence of benefit*. This element includes demonstrable evidence of the innovation's advantages, including cost, time, quality, and customer satisfaction. We derive this model inductively and iteratively from the ethnographic material.

Intimate apparel firm

Looking within silos: "Bras don't talk to panties"

The intimate apparel firm was a bricolage of brands that had once been independent. Managers, merchandisers, planners, and sales staff had not previously been housed under the same roof prior to spinning off from a holding company about 5 years before our study began. Management resided on the fifth floor at the top of the office building, recapitulating in physical space the social and power distance between upper management and all other employees. Brand managers, planners, and other workers inhabited the corporate workspaces, laden with racks of sample products and display prototypes, spread out on the third floor of the building. Designers were located in the historic garment district in New York, more than an hour away by plane from corporate headquarters.

While there were several other work units corresponding to specialty products like men's underwear and so-called "active wear" designed for exercise, sport, and outdoor activities, the two key players in our study were the bra department and the women's panty department. These two groups had separate managers. Bras were the profit center for the company and included old-line brands dating from the late 1920s, one that emerged in the 1940s, and a well-known figure-enhancing "push-up" line that emerged in the mid-1950s. Each bra line had its associated line of panties but the panty lines responded to the color and fabric choices that were set by the leadership in the bra division.

Although bras and panties were located next to one another, tension between the two product categories was frequently mentioned by the panty-group members and by sales and field service staffers. One newly hired manager said, "We don't meet with panties, and we don't meet with other bras. They are on my floor, but we are not talking among ourselves. We don't feel we are competing, but we don't talk about what worked well... . It is kind of a silo here." A member of one of the bra teams said that they work well as product teams (within their silos), but between teams (across silos) they work "very independently of each other, too." She went on: "It's not competitive or anything, but we are so different from one another." Packaging or labeling issues were resolved at the brand level, and coordination among and between brands, like the interaction among and between bras and panties, was infrequent and guided by individual initiative. These bra and panty teams worked separately on projects for their individual brands, were ultimately responsible for the sales results that stemmed from their departments, and had to get permission from higher-ranking leaders for any product changes. Even when teams wanted to communicate or transfer (e.g., ideas, product) across different teams (or "businesses" or "worlds" as some people called them), they couldn't. One member said, "We can't. Everyone still has different systems. It's like transferring to a different company."

While we cannot describe the organization as a whole since it includes complex international supply chain units and other brands that were not the focus of our study, we do know that in women's intimates, matching sets was an issue for many shoppers and for many managers. Product development, point-of-sale merchandising, and manufacturing variation (e.g., dye-lot, fabrics, garment construction) were implicated in the differences between bras and panties. Bras are more difficult and expensive to produce than are panties, and offer the company higher margins. Bras are most often sold on hangers at retail; panties are generally packaged – though the competition offers "table programs" from which shoppers can mix and match individual panties laid out on a table, and some of the company's outlet stores offer this option. Although these products are made differently, in different manufacturing plants, those differences are attenuated at retail and in the consumer's experience. Surprisingly, in-store mannequins generally featured matching sets in both company-owned stores and in department stores like Macy's, and point-of-sale information, such as garment tags and packaging graphics, often featured matching sets, suggesting that the company was both driving and responding to a customer preference. At one flagship department store in New York, matching sets had been put on mannequins only to be taken down; the store was unable to obtain enough matching sets from the manufacturer. For at least some of the company's bra and panties lines, a limited number of matching sets were available so some coordination across categories was evidently taking place. But at retail, they were rarely in stock where and when customers wanted them.

We heard similar issues from managers working with an allied direct-sales organization that featured women's intimate wear in their catalogue offerings, and the same concerns from online sales managers. They could not get enough matching sets. Some managers felt matching sets were really important, while others, primarily upper management, did not seem to see them as a priority. The inability of different corporate units to develop and market bras and panties in a more coordinated way also was reflected in the spatial layout of the sales floor. Intimate apparel departments have separate sections for bras and panties; within those sections, our intimate apparel firm would have its bras displayed separately from its panties. In addition, the inability to both find and purchase matching sets was reflected in the frustrating experiences reported to us by women during the in-home interviews; these women were the ones who were ultimately affected by both the silo-ed organizational structure of the firm, the decision to offer only limited runs of matching sets, and the difficulty of finding those matching sets at retail. One of our in-home interviewees encountered this problem and commented with both surprise and annoyance, "Why can't a big company like this figure out how to manufacture enough matching sets?"

Looking across silos: Keeping a lid on the silos helps maintain the status quo

Although the product moved from manufacturing through marketing, distribution, and in-store placement with carefully aligned point-of-sale materials and promotional schemes, information about what was happening along this value chain depended on the openness of borders between organizational units. Sales teams engaged in cross-functional meetings and idea sharing with one another and with the merchandisers whose product was available in the stores that each sales person supported. But these sales professionals also acknowledged that bras and panties, and different kinds of bras, "do not do cross-functional meetings." One sales staffer said that although he had been there for more than 5 years, he could not talk directly with a designer. Instead, he was required to talk to someone in merchandising, who would contact the designers. "The designers," he said, "will design what they think is right." Even when management teams have design ideas and push them up to New York, their concepts are not well received. It is, we were told, "pushback from the designers as to why they couldn't do it." Little if any cross-functional teaming occurred unless it related to production runs and general product availability.

Listening to customers, however, is part of the daily job for two kinds of staff: Store managers who operate the company's own outlet stores that are scattered around the United States, and "field support" team members who are responsible for visiting the big-box and mid-tier retailers. Tellingly, there is no formal communication opportunity between these two customer-focused groups. The retail store managers gain a high degree of awareness through their daily interaction with customers in their stores. Their concerns, drawn from a separate study, included the difficulty of obtaining matching sets. As one manager pointed out, "One of the things we can improve on is bra/panties sets to match... . People love to have matching sets."

The field support team is in direct contact with retail customers but there is no institutionalized way of drawing upon their insights for the product and marketing strategies that are in play at headquarters. The role of the team includes tasks such as making sure that displays are correctly set, that local retailers get their questions answered, and that local promotions are correctly implemented. When working on a display in a store, field support staffers take pride in visiting with customers, helping them with fit and style selection, and doing their best to act as in-store sales staff. The manager of this group, who said her input was not part of higher level management discussions, calculated that about 40 percent of her group's time was spent selling product to women at retail. When this manager began working for the company, she had a $14 million budget and over 300 staffers. At the time of the study, she had less than half the money and 177 staffers. Her staff does not have computers and they file their reports on paper – something that she hopes to change. She stated, "The [field support] staff was there to put out stock and not think about the customer." However, she wants her staff focused on customer needs and on selling. Input from this manager's team was not seen or used as a resource. She stated, "No one uses our group as much as they should."

One other example of cross-silo interaction involved two different silos: sales and bras. One high-level sales person, call him Jim, was frustrated with the complexity of the bra offerings he was pushing out to the big-box retailers. He pulled out a bra from one of the lines in which he had done well in a prior year and asked that the bra be scaled up to fit larger women; larger sizes were an important part of the target consumer in big-box retail. The woman in charge of the old bra, call her Emily, did not see a benefit in a restyling and up-sizing since the brand was not sold in big-box retail. In other words, increased sales would not benefit her bottom line. Her colleague, whose products were sold in big-box, responded that she would have to talk to Emily whose bras were sold "upstairs" in department stores and not in the lower-priced big-box retail space. Emily was the manager who had just told the sales executive Jim that his idea was not of interest. In response, Jim said he "went over their heads" and took his idea to the division manager who moved the idea of the scaled-up bra forward in 12 months and shaved 6 months off the usual product-development cycle. "I'm throwing years of credit out the window if I fail. My ass is on the line. Not a lot of people will walk out on a limb." Jim ended the story by saying that the company "will ship 250,000 units of that bra" in the current year. Leapfrogging silos in this way demonstrates the absence of institutionalized systems for sharing information and taking action in response to market needs.

Intimates' mixed outcomes

The intimate apparel company sees its greatest margins from sales of products that are packaged in plastic like panties and sold at big-box retail as a commodity. Yet our research showed broad dissatisfaction not only with the difficulty of finding matching panty and bra sets, but also with finding the combination and correct size, style, and color. The only people who enjoyed shopping for bras were those who could afford shopping at high-end boutiques or those younger consumers who were Victoria Secret loyalists. It seemed the intimate apparel firm had a formula that was meeting its financial needs without having to address the serious organizational challenges presented by (1) sewing together formerly independent brands, (2) linking the highly independent design teams with the teams responsible for merchandising, marketing, and selling, and (3) gathering and using input from interface units (e.g., field support, online, outlet stores) and shoppers. The outcomes related to the innovations were not all negative, but they did not allow timely response to market needs. Some matching sets were available, some of the time, so there must have been some collaboration. However, the firm did not make enough of them because they weren't committed to the concept. One recent earnings report from the company indicated that in recent years there has been an effort to move away from the commodity-based approach, and to upgrade the panty programs, generally, and they say this has been successful. While we were there, consistent and institutionalized pathways out of the silo-ed bra/panty world simply did not exist.

Global vehicle program

Looking within silos: Organizational processes and practices vary

The initial interview with a marketing manager offered a window into GM's organizational-culture differences which coincided with its silo-ed corporate structure. The marketing manager was affiliated with Adam Opel AG, the German-based engineering unit involved in the global program. He commented, "You should have been at that meeting today; it was a classic! I've had such a terrible morning. I'll have to tell you about it. It's just so frustrating!" He brought up two issues. First, he pointed out that in Europe, people:

try to get things done in a quick, direct way. Everyone here (in the U.S.) tries to hide behind a process. The process tells you what step to do next. In Germany, we go to A or B to get something done and if that doesn't work, we do it ourselves. I've seen a lot of people put up processes and not follow them at all in the U.S. We need to learn about processes but we need to produce results.

He quickly followed with another comment about the American-run meetings he had been attending that were "completely unorganized with no purpose." This manager was used to a formal meeting agenda which would include "what decision you want made" based on a "one pager" submitted well in advance of the meeting. At these meetings, minutes were taken. When meeting attendees later received the minutes, all decisions were summarized (see Ferraro & Briody, 2013, pp. 166–172.)

In subsequent discussions with program participants, it became clear that the purpose of meetings, the content covered, their format or style, and the amount of time allocated to them differed by engineering unit. For example, Small Car Group, one of the American units, preferred spending most of the workweek in meetings since that was where information was shared and issues discussed. However, the other American unit, Saturn, preferred to keep meeting times to a minimum and to use a focused format and agenda for developing consensus on issues. All three units spent some time each week working independently to ensure that their customer requirements were part of their vehicles and to strategize how those requirements should be incorporated into the vehicle underbody.

Over a period of a few months, the interview and observation data also revealed that each of the three engineering organizations employed a particular decision-making model. Small Car Group used an adaptation of the majority-rule model known as *majority preferred*. Individuals would "pitch" their ideas, advocating for their views in the hopes of securing "buy in" from other members and the unit's leader. Individualism was quite important to this overall process. The majority viewpoint typically prevailed unless the engineering leader opted for an alternative.

Saturn's decision-making model was based on *100-percent consensus*. All engineering unit members had to "buy in" to a particular decision or there was no decision. Important to this unit were notions of equality and democracy. It could take a significant amount of time to review all the input and align all member views. To assist with that process, members used the following rule of thumb: If you are 70 percent comfortable with a particular decision, you must state that you are "in," meaning you are in favor of the decision. In the event that the engineering groups were unable to reach consensus, they would approach a higher-ranking group within Saturn to assist them with the decision.

Opel's model was largely dependent on what the "leader" decided. Known as the *leadership-driven* model, it was the leader's responsibility to make the call. (Leaders, of course, were present at all levels of the hierarchy and had varying levels of authority based on their role.) Nonetheless, decisions were not made in a vacuum. Instead, the leader solicited input from various sources. Program participants indicated that they were able to offer their perspectives or an assessment of a particular proposal freely and honestly if they were asked; they supported their views based on "data" they had compiled. They did not offer input if they were not asked (see Briody, Cavusgil, and Stewart 2004, pp. 426–428).

Looking across silos: Low levels of cohesion and authority challenge collaboration

The challenges of a global vehicle program emerged only when two or more of the three engineering groups began working together. The Opel meeting style clashed with what the Germans perceived as the "American" meeting style. Initially, the meeting differences appeared to be largely an annoyance that created tension and communication difficulties. However, as the three units found that they had to interface more frequently and regularly, their differences resulted in work practice disruption. Program participants seemed at a loss for how to run program meetings when more than one engineering unit was present. The default way was that associated with Small Car Group which was considered the "program lead." This unit had the highest status and the greatest power on the program because (1) it contributed about 80 percent of the vehicle program's members; (2) its car would be the first to roll off the assembly line, followed at 18-month intervals by the cars of the other two units; and (3) its leader was assigned the role of program manager for the entire program.

Decision-making differences only added to the difficulties and contributed to low levels of cohesion among program participants. No one seemed to understand that each engineering unit had its own assumptions about how decisions were made. Instead, participants only recognized that decision making was painful and wondered why the others did not "think" like they did. Moreover, it was almost impossible to get all three units to reach agreement on a particular decision. Sometimes two of the engineering units would agree and attempt to force the third unit to comply. The latter would be challenged to "put on the (program's) hat," meaning that it should "be a team player" and go along with the majority view.

The reaction by the dissenting unit typically included an explanation for why it was unable to comply with the proposed decision. For example, Opel often used marketing data to point out differences in customer expectations and justify the fallacy of global programs. The dissenting unit would then seek the support of its own senior leaders to intervene on its behalf and reverse the "decision." Often high-ranking senior leaders of the dissenting unit would agree. If the other two engineering units continued their pressure to conform to the majority view, the dissenting unit's senior leaders would make a credible threat to "pull out of the program." Such a threat undermined the authority of the program manager and threw the program into a period of ambiguity and uncertainty. Developing cross-unit collaboration and a team spirit was inhibited as team members realized that appeals could be made through their respective chains of command.

A high profile example of this type of conflict involved moving the cowl forward (i.e., the top portion of the vehicle body attached to the windshield). This issue appeared as the vehicle program approached its first "Concept Initiation" milestone, a key decision point in the product development process. Opel's marketing arm was concerned that the car's styling would look "outdated" and would not be able to compete successfully with one particular group of Mercedes vehicles. The Opel proposal was to move the cowl forward by 75 mm. As one of the German employees stated,

> (The vehicle program) was close to being canceled. (The program manager and the lead engineer for Opel) were told there was one chance: if they changed the styling to (be like the Mercedes) vehicles, maybe Opel could stay in. (Opel's) marketing pushed it and won.... (The program manager and the lead engineer for Opel) agreed to it in Germany and they let us know by phone calls. They were forced to make a decision.

In the first few weeks following the decision to move the cowl forward, work was done to estimate the engineering and timing impact of this architectural change. Continued discussion of the pros and cons of the change ensued over several weeks. Finally, the program manager was reported to have intervened, stating, "This decision has been made." At about the same time, a senior German leader visiting from Germany, commented, "(The cowl forward change) suits us all." These statements by both the program manager and the senior German leader signaled that this particular issue had been settled.

A failed experiment

The decision-making dilemmas that plagued GM's global vehicle program had important effects. First, management credibility was called into question when the template for the vehicle program system was inconsistent with day-to-day realities. This template emphasized the role of the program manager as a "strong program manager," establishing expectations that all vehicle programs would be managed differently than they had been in the past. Senior leadership intervention violated the envisioned global program structure in which the program manager was "accountable for the program's profitability and performance." When program personnel and others beyond the program saw that the template was largely disregarded in favor of the traditional autonomy and authority of the individual (silo-ed) units, they judged the new vehicle program structure quite harshly. The vehicle program template was branded as just another "program of the month."

Second, decision-making delays resulted, rendering the program's mantra "timing is sacred" largely meaningless. Decision-making delays were the result of the changeable authority of the program manager over product decisions and disregard for the product development process. The vehicle program team, faced with numerous threats of program cancellation, had to revisit, and then remake, decisions. There did not appear to be any particular mechanism to resolve an issue "once and for all" other than invoking the senior leadership of the firm. Revisiting issues, time after time, took attention and focus away from newly emerging technical and business issues. The result was that the program was delayed, thereby lengthening, not reducing, lead time. In the case of the cowl forward issue, the program lost 6 months due to the extent of rework on the architectural changes; it also added a significant increase in the program's costs. (See Briody, 2010 for another example.)

Approximately 2 years after the global vehicle program was initiated, it ended. First one and then the second engineering unit made the decision to "pull out" of the program, thus rendering the concept of a global partnership and cross-silo collaboration a failure. It was a high-stakes experiment that cost the corporation an estimated $2.2 million vehicle sales, threatened the long-term viability of global vehicle programs, and called into question the corporation's future as a global manufacturer.

Hospital

Looking within silos: Choices are made locally

A recent innovation for the hospital targeted staff–patient interaction; implementation was anticipated to be hospital-wide. AIDET (in which A = Acknowledge, I = Introduce, D = Duration, E = Explanation, and T = Thank You) was an acronym for a communication tool to help staff in their interactions with patients. Human Resource managers had introduced AIDET to middle management and some senior management during a leadership retreat; attendees were required to roll it out to their staff. A few months later, new hires were exposed to AIDET during their orientation.

Approximately 1 year after the leadership retreat, AIDET had been fully embraced by only two hospital units which reported to the Chief Operating Officer (though many other units also reported to him). EVS (Environmental Services) and Dietary incorporated AIDET into their daily interactions with patients. They were led by an energetic EVS manager who was supported by her middle manager; her manager also oversaw dietary. She regularly reinforced the learning and use of AIDET through individual and group practice, discussion at meetings, and small laminated cards as reminders of the acronym. The EVS and dietary staff expressed their acceptance of AIDET through statements such as "It is part of our life (here)" and "(It) helps patients understand who you are and makes them feel welcome." Later, this same energetic EVS manager helped extend Plant Engineering's use of AIDET by helping to adapt AIDET for use in interactions with nursing floor staff.

Reactions to AIDET by those working in non-compliant departments and floors varied. One staff member commented, "Just another stupid customer service program – won't be effective until our culture changes." A second offered, "Reviewed several weeks ago and don't remember the material." A third stated, "It is not applicable to my job duties," while a fourth indicated, "I like it but I don't think we need to be waking the patients up to do AIDET." Yet, staff members who participated in a cross-silo patient experience team and who were involved in the training and assessment of AIDET use found the rollout of the innovation problematic. There seemed to be no willingness to require staff to use it. As much as they tried to push this innovation for over one year, their efforts fell short. AIDET adoption was not successful throughout the hospital. There was no hospital-wide mandate or set of incentives for using AIDET to help structure staff–patient interactions, nor was there any enforcement across the hospital silos by senior hospital leadership to use it. Indeed, there was no agreement on the value of AIDET. Comments on patient satisfaction surveys indicated patients' appreciation when staff interacted with them in friendly and empathetic ways, and dissatisfaction when they did not.

Communication is not only experienced face to face, such as in AIDET-based conversations, but also through experiences. Patient satisfaction surveys revealed the effect of wait time and delays: They resulted in negative perceptions of the hospital. Patient flow, the movement of patients to get the care they need in the hospital setting, has long been an issue at the hospital due to bottlenecks, staff shortages, and other issues. Combatting the patient flow problem occurred primarily within silos. For example, the Emergency Room (ER) introduced "direct bedding" in which the patient would bypass triage and go straight to an ER bed; triage would happen at the bedside. Nursing floors would bring on additional staff through the "float pool" or share staffing. Staff might pitch in and perform certain roles that they did not usually do (e.g., take a patient down for discharge).

However, staff reactions often included "blaming" and "finger pointing" as they expressed their frustration with those upstream units who turned patients over to them. The ER, in particular, was often the target of the blame. For example, one staff member stated, "Between 6:00–7:00 p.m. which is our change of shift, they want to send four patients up (to Unit X).... Well, damn it, patient flow has to do with the safety of.... We can't handle them!" The ER's actions, and subsequent actions on the floors, had downstream effects. An EVS staff member commented, "I don't think the floors understand ... that when they have five patients that are set for discharge and they put all five patients in the computer minutes after each other, how that really affects the flow from an EVS standpoint." In this example, EVS would be notified all at once that five beds were waiting to be cleaned.

Looking across silos: Leadership support and incentives can foster collaboration

To help reduce patient wait time, the ER re-established the mission of the Admission, Discharge, and Transfer (ADT) Unit. While the ADT had long been a unit of the hospital, it had been used most recently as an overflow unit after surgical procedures. After a restructuring in which the ADT became part of the ER, ER management conducted a series of pilot studies demonstrating significant reductions in patient wait time and improved patient satisfaction when the ADT was used for its intended purpose. Prior to that point, patients could remain in the ER for up to 20 hours, 8 hours on average, depending on hospital capacity and census. One of the ER managers told us,

> Our goal is to get those patients out of the ER. If that patient needs to be admitted and is stable, they can come up to the ADT unit. A physician will meet them there. The patient is in a private room. They are in a medical bed. They are allowed to have family.… . And the staff up there will watch you and communicate … (and) it opens up a bed in the ER for the patient in the waiting room. The next patient has somewhere to go.

Two aspects of the ADT required cross-silo collaboration. First, ancillary units serving the ADT agreed to provide the same quick turnaround times on diagnostic tests that they offered the ER staff; securing the physicians' agreement was critical to getting the ADT up and running. One of the ER managers told us,

> I met with every manager before starting this study and said, "Here's our plans. This is where we need to go." And all of them were receptive – the pharmacy, radiology, lab. I said, "We're going to have extra taxing stuff on you. We're going to expect you to turn over these orders relatively quick. This is going to add a huge workload burden on you. Is this something you're willing to do?" None of them blinked an eye at it. They all said, "Let's go for it." They've all jumped in and tackled the issue. It's been a group effort.

Second, the ER managers created an additional ADT service called the "roving nurse." One of the managers commented, "That nurse goes through the house (any hospital floor) and … facilitate(s) discharges. If we're at 100 percent capacity, that nurse tags another nurse usually provided by float pool. And there's two nurses now roving around… . So they are averaging about 12 discharges a day." In turn, the "roving nurses" help free up the floors.

The repurposing of the ADT did create tension with other hospital units. Staff were used to using the ADT as a "holdover area" when the hospital's census was high; eventually that option was no longer a possibility. Some nursing floors refused to have the roving nurses assist them with discharges and, at the same time, chose not to send their discharged patients down to the ADT lounge to wait for family members for pick up. However, the managers had strong support within their chain of command. Over time such resistance lessened because "the floors are graded on how long it takes to get a patient out of the door so they see the roving nurses as a help to that process," one of the managers explained. Even members of the hospital's senior leadership, who were initially skeptical, ultimately accepted the ADT because it proved to be cost effective.

Some promising results

The ADT innovation fared far better than that of AIDET and resulted in the collaboration of multiple hospital units led by mid-level ER management. Their pilot studies and extensive experimentation with days and hours of operation over a long period of time resulted in a reasonably smooth restructuring. Over the course of its first few months of operation, the ADT was able to demonstrate continued reductions in patient wait time, more efficient and effective patient care, and improved hospital experiences.

One of the ER managers anticipated that if the ADT restructuring worked, it would be possible to create other similar cross-silo collaborations within the hospital. He reported

> We're really excited about it. And to me the exciting part is not just looking at what the ADT is capable of doing – is that I know we can replicate that anywhere in the building. And that's my ultimate vision of this … to say, 'Yeah, we did it over here but you can do it over there.'

His belief has been borne out by other significant organizational innovations – all involving the ER and all leading to faster and better patient care. In all of these initiatives, multiple units had to participate to ensure success.

The most recent of these initiatives was launched after both ER managers had been promoted – one to head all of nursing operations and the other to head the ER and serve as the lead for the patient flow initiative. Together they were in a position to extend their focus on patient flow from the ER to the nursing floors. They gathered estimates from each floor of the number of beds they would need (e.g., based on anticipated admissions, surgeries, other procedures) during the busy nights mid-week. Initially the floors resisted compiling and providing this information. However, with the constant focus of these managers during afternoon "rounding," their clear expectations to the floors, good-natured interactions, and follow up with the "daily scorecard" to highlight improvements, resistance gave way to acceptance. The new nursing operations manager, in speaking with one of the floor staff said, "We're going to give you the support and resources… . If you see something that's not working, come back to me and let me know."

The two managers convened a small, cross-silo team which included nursing, ER, EVS, and others, to project the number of beds that would be needed at night and determine the appropriate number and type of staff to care for those patients. Staff participating in this Nightly Bed Projection Team found the problem-solving work to be engaging and empowering. They even turned their predictions into a game, making it into a fun activity. New members rotated into this team, thereby quickly broadening the staff's overall knowledge base. Over time, confidence grew in the value of the team's projections and the ability to plan accurately for staffing needs. This "data driven" approach helped to remove much of the uncertainty that the floors faced. Moreover, the team was able to show that the number of patient comments related to wait time and the percentage of negative comments overall declined following the launch of the nightly bed projection meetings.

Innovation paths

In this section we explore what can happen internally within a silo, and organizationally across silos, as innovations are introduced. These cross-silo interactions had different progressions or paths and led to different innovation outcomes. For each of the 10 paths below, we describe and depict the sequence of key organizational-culture features associated with each path.

Paths to innovation failure

Six of the paths resulted in innovation failure. They included the Global Vehicle Program path, the four paths taken to establish Matching Sets as part of the intimate apparel product line, and one of the AIDET paths.

Global vehicle program

The senior leadership came up with the idea for a global program, expecting that three of their engineering units would be able to work together. Yet, internal cohesion suffered as a result of differences in work practices and processes (e.g., meeting styles, decision-making models) and the seizure of authority from the program manager. Collaborations did form over specific engineering issues, but they were short-lived, only to be replaced by different alliances on other engineering issues. Resistance soared as senior leaders intervened in program matters, ultimately confirming that none of the three engineering units would be able to engineer its car models to appeal to its customer base. Any hope of achieving global economies of scale was dashed and the expectation that the three silo-ed units would become a collaborative and integrated global program was never realized (see Figure 3.2).

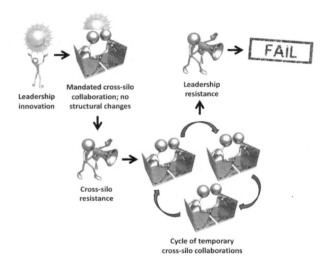

Figure 3.2 The Global Vehicle Program's path to innovation failure. (Image courtesy of Elizabeth Briody.)

Matching sets #1

We identified four paths associated with attempts to collaborate on matching sets of bras and panties. Only one of the four paths experienced any success: some number of matching bras and panties were produced and sold. This effort required cross-silo collaboration throughout the product development process and in retail and online sales and marketing. At some point, leadership resistance to matching sets increased and they were never produced in sufficient quantities given the demand. When we interviewed executives, we received only a lukewarm reaction to matching sets. Interestingly, sales and marketing have continued to show models and mannequins wearing matching sets. Ultimately, this path resulted in failure (see Figure 3.3). As of this writing, bras and panties are only offered separately on the company's website. We found no matching sets.

Matching sets #2

Among corporate employees, we found that cross-silo collaboration was envisioned but never materialized. Employees told us that they could not understand why there was not more teamwork among the bra and panty silos. Instead, employees found that they remained largely isolated within their own silos, which in effect prevented them from working together on joint projects such as matching sets. Corporate management resisted making a commitment to robust and ongoing cross-silo collaboration (see Figure 3.4).

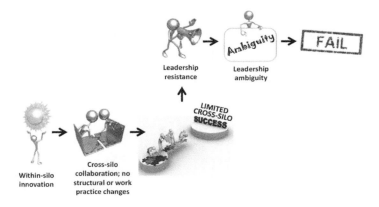

Figure 3.3 A partial success for matching sets leads eventually to failure. (Image courtesy of Elizabeth Briody.)

Figure 3.4 Corporate employees fail in raising the question "Why no matching sets?" (Image courtesy of Elizabeth Briody.)

Matching sets #3

Another path consisted of input from customers to "front line" employees such as those who worked in field services or in online sales. Our interviews with front-line employees revealed that customers with whom they spoke commented on the lack of availability of matching sets. Such customer input was passed along to the managers of these front-line employees where it typically received no traction (see Figure 3.5).

Figure 3.5 Front-line employees fail in passing along customer feedback. (Image courtesy of Elizabeth Briody.)

Matching sets #4

A final path involved our research team. Corporate as well as front-line employees shared their views with us on matching sets, as did store sales associates, and the many customers we interviewed. We sensed their keen frustration about an insufficient supply to meet demand. We reported these views and our recommendations to the management group sponsoring our project. As far as we know, no action was taken (see Figure 3.6).

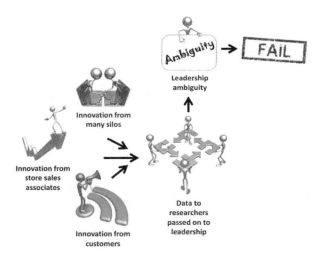

Figure 3.6 Research team advocacy fails to make the case for matching sets. (Image courtesy of Elizabeth Briody.)

AIDET #1

Our research team observed a predominant reaction to AIDET after hospital mid-level and senior management were exposed to it. A large number of hospital silos – particularly those in the business functions – kept their views on AIDET out of the public realm. Clinical care silos also seemed to ignore this initiative either because they believed their approach to patient care was already exceptional or because they did not value what AIDET offered. Over time these noncompliant units were able to disengage from the attempted AIDET implementation. We also noted that senior hospital leadership did not routinely mention AIDET in their communications; rarely did we hear them refer to it. Thus, leadership ambiguity characterized the bulk of the response to this innovation, which ultimately led to its demise (see Figure 3.7).

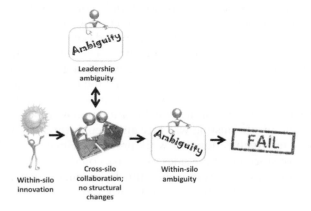

Figure 3.7 Ambiguity surrounding AIDET tied to innovation failure. (Image courtesy of Elizabeth Briody.)

Paths to partial realization of innovation

Two of the 10 paths represented a partial success in terms of innovation path outcome. In one other AIDET path, the outcome represented a subsystem success. Employees in nonclinical roles with direct patient contact changed the way in which they interacted with patients. A second example of a partial success involved the scaled-up bra. Its accomplishments were limited to a one-time-only success.

AIDET #2

Unlike the ambiguous reception AIDET received in most hospital silos, some silos fully accepted it. EVS and dietary services incorporated AIDET into their daily tasks. Their leaders conducted group training, on-on-one practice sessions with employees, and follow-up evaluations. These leaders also created incentives to reward employees who put this innovation to use. Members of the EVS and dietary silos received positive feedback from patients through direct verbal feedback as well as written comments on patient satisfaction surveys. One other silo, plant engineering, took note of EVS and dietary's achievements and received help applying AIDET to interactions with nursing staff (see Figure 3.8). While successful across selected silos, AIDET was never extended system-wide.

Scaled-up bra

We were told that it takes roughly 18 months to move a bra from the idea stage to placement on intimate department retail shelves. Doing so in about a year, as was the case with the re-sized and rebranded department store offering, did not come about because of an effort by management to bridge silos. It was done by breaking rank. It happened only after a high-level sales executive got no buy-in from the bra units. The innovation was pushed through when the executive who managed both bra groups agreed with the sales executive and took on the project. While the new bra was selling well, the innovation did not produce any organizational change and may have damaged relationships and future collaboration potential between cross-silo peers. This kind of silo-busting was rare and seen as threatening by some. It also produced no organizational or work practice changes other than adding to the corpus of stories that the sales executive could tell about the difficulty the organization has with responsive, timely product innovation. System-wide innovation was not achieved (see Figure 3.9).

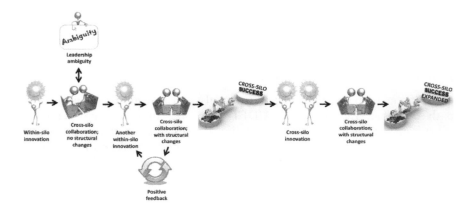

Figure 3.8 AIDET's successful integration within some hospital silos. (Image courtesy of Elizabeth Briody.)

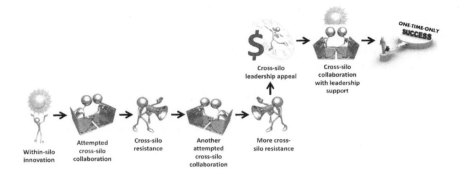

Figure 3.9 The one-time-only success of the scaled-up bra. (Image courtesy of Elizabeth Briody.)

Paths to innovation success

We identified two paths to successful system-wide innovation among our group of 10. Both successes were part of hospital operations and led by the same middle management leaders. We identified within-silo, chain-of-command support for both innovations. Resistance emerged during the innovation process but was addressed.

ADT

Two ER middle managers were able to secure agreement from their senior leader to test out the ADT concept once a restructuring placed the ADT under the control of the ER. They approached all ancillary units to see if those units would be able to collaborate with the ADT and provide quick turnaround time on diagnostic tests. With the ancillary units' support, the ADT began its pilots. Most nursing floor resisted the help of the ADT's roving nurses until the floors were subjected to discharge metrics. Some senior leaders also resisted the ADT innovation arguing that it would not be cost effective; once the cost issue was overcome, senior leadership resistance weakened. At that point, the cross-silo collaborations between the ER and the ancillary units, and the ADT's roving nurses and the nursing floors, were able to get the full value out of the ADT innovation (see Figure 3.10).

Nightly bed projection team

This innovative team was created by the two middle managers who had led the ADT innovation and had been subsequently promoted. Now part of two different silos, the pair got support from the senior leader to whom they both reported. However, the two individuals then faced some initial resistance by the large silo composed of nursing floors; their request to the floors for anticipated and confirmed discharges was unusual and created additional work. They were able to break down this resistance by building relationships with the key nursing staff on each floor, and by taking the time to explain how the floors would benefit from the innovation. Soon the floors demonstrated their collaboration by having the numbers ready when the two made their rounds. With the floors' input, it was then possible for the Nightly Bed Projection Team to develop their projections, share them with other units (e.g., patient transportation, EVS), and determine the most accurate staffing ratios for the night. This system-wide innovation is ongoing (see Figure 3.11).

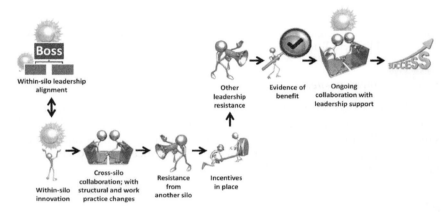

Figure 3.10 The path to ADT's innovation-wide success. (Image courtesy of Elizabeth Briody.)

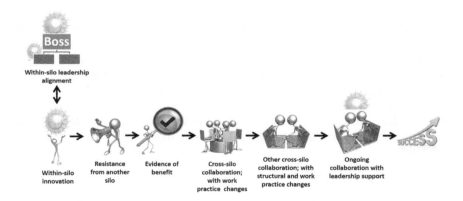

Figure 3.11 The successful innovation-wide path involving the Nightly Bed Projection Team. (Image courtesy of Elizabeth Briody.)

Organization culture and innovation outcomes

Our ethnographic exploration of the 10 paths provides both insight and nuance into innovation in silo-ed organizations. We created Table 3.1 as a tool to aid our understanding of the innovation process. Table 3.1 incorporates the five organizational-culture features modeled in Figure 3.1: collaboration, leadership buy-in, structural change, work practice change, and evidence of benefit. Table 3.1 also includes the innovation path outcomes and the system-wide innovation outcomes. (Our analysis can be explored or tested for robustness by other researchers using alternate data sets, whether ethnographic or not.)

None of the five features listed in Table 3.1 presents a simple, straightforward, linear, explanation. Collaboration, for example, appears early (AIDET #1) as well as late (scaled-up bra) during the innovation process. Sometimes it is mandated (global vehicle program) and sometimes it is not (ADT). Sometimes it lasts (AIDET #2) and sometimes it is short lived (matching sets #1). Sometimes it is temporary or sporadic (global vehicle program) and sometimes it is a constant (ADT). And, sometimes it never occurs (matching sets #2, #3, and #4) while in other instances it emerges stronger after resistance has been overcome (Nightly Bed Projection Team).

The four remaining organizational-culture features also reveal a messy complexity. We see that if leadership buy-in wavers or is ambiguous, rather than being stable and clear, system-wide success is not achieved. If structural changes do not accompany the innovation, the implementation of the innovation is unlikely. Work practice changes also are important to innovation success. In the case of the ADT, the enforcement of the metrics related to discharge time forced a change in work practices; only then were nursing floors willing to accept the help of the roving nurses. Finally, when there is no obvious benefit to the innovation, the implementation of that innovation is unlikely. In fact, even if there is a documented benefit – such as in AIDET #2 – the innovation may not expand system-wide. This pattern was confirmed recently at the hospital. Approximately 18 months after the introduction of AIDET, there is no longer any push to adopt it. As of this writing, one of the hospital managers indicated, "I hear very little from anyone about AIDET."

Table 3.1 illustrates that all five organizational-culture features are important to successful system-wide innovation in silo-ed organizations. These five features are associated with the two successes – the ADT and the Nightly Bed Projection Team.

By contrast, one or more of these features is missing in all remaining innovations. The innovations that we designated as partial successes incorporated some of these features during the innovation. For example, the scaled-up bra was produced through a collaborative appeal to leadership authority. However, this innovation did not represent a permanent change in either organizational structure or work practices, and damaged the

Table 3.1 Opportunities for innovation by selected organizational-culture features and outcomes. (Courtesy of Elizabeth Briody.)

Cases and Innovation Paths	Collaboration	Leadership Buy-In	Structural Change	Work Practice Change	Evidence of Benefit	Innovation Path Outcome	System-Wide Innovation
Global Vehicle Program	Mandated; then occasionally, issue by issue	Only at outset; then decreased over time	No, due to insufficient changes, so silos reinforced	No	No	Failure	Failure
Matching Sets #1	Some, but short lived	Only at outset; then decreased over time	No	No	Unclear	Limited cross-silo success; then failure	
Matching Sets #2 Failure	No	No	No	No	No	Failure	
Matching Sets #3	No	No	No	No	No	Failure	
Matching Sets #4	No	No	No	No	No	Failure	
AIDET #1	Yes	Ambiguous	No	No	No	Failure	
AIDET #2	Yes	Only certain silos; others ambiguous	Only certain silos	Only certain silos	Yes	Ongoing success across selected silos	Partial Success
Scaled-Up Bra	Not initially	Only a particular leadership silo	Not initially	Not initially	No	One-time only success	Partial Success
ADT	Yes	Initially only innovating silo's leadership; then resistance by all others; finally buy-in by all	Yes	Not until metrics enforced	Yes	Success	Success
Nightly Bed Projection	Yes after resistance	Initially certain silos; then later	Yes	Yes	Yes	Success	Success

potential for future collaboration with peers. Consequently, it was not sustainable in the long run.

The majority of the innovations were failures. For example, the global vehicle program floundered on all five features. Collaboration lasted only as long as it took to secure agreement on a technical issue. Structural mechanisms were inadequate to ensure program authority and no incentives were in place to create a cohesive team. Leadership buy-in, unexpectedly, increased the internal conflict and contributed to the program's termination. Finally, no evidence could be found that the global vehicle program innovation would lead to long-term success in its current configuration.

Conclusions

Silos are capable of producing work within their own areas of routine expertise and can be both proficient and resourceful in getting their own work done. They help cut back on the "noise" or distractions from other units which can limit their efficiency. But when action is required that involves sharing, coordination, and cooperation across silos, particularly in response to external environmental change, silo boundaries become a problem to be solved.

Silo-ed organizations follow different paths when attempting to implement change. Sometimes different paths emerge associated with the same innovative idea. One or more of these paths might yield some success, although that success might be temporary or confined to a particular part of the organization. System-wide change involves a more comprehensive approach, more effort, and more organizational members to ensure it is successful. The variation in system-wide change is based on such elements as who initiates the innovative idea, the perceived priority and beneficiaries of the innovation, aligned leadership and employee support, complexities associated with workplace restructurings and changes in the nature of work, and the ease with which value from the innovation can be identified.

Cross-silo collaboration can and does happen; when it does, the boundaries between silos become less salient and in-group versus out-group differences and conflict are weakened. Collaboration seems to work best when expectations about it are embedded within the organization's cultural rules, and when mechanisms are in place to support it. Yet, while collaboration is a necessary condition, it is not a sufficient condition to ensure system-wide success. Our data suggest that collaboration that occurs in concert or in tandem with four other organizational-culture features – leadership buy-in, structural change, work practice change, and evidence of benefit – leads to system-wide success. When those five elements are not present, it is likely that any success will be partial at best.

Acknowledgments

We appreciate the comments we received from Maryann McCabe, Robin Beers, and Marc S. Robinson. Their ideas and suggestions helped to make the chapter stronger.

References

Aaker, D. (2013). *Spanning Silos: The New CMO Imperative*. Cambridge, MA: Harvard Business Press.

Bandali, K., B. Niblett, T. P. C., Yeung, and P. Gamble. (2011). Beyond Curriculum: Embedding Interprofessional Collaboration into Academic Culture. *Journal of Interprofessional Care*, 25, 75–76.

Bannister, F. (2001). Dismantling the Silos: Extracting New Value from IT Investments in Public Administration. *Information Systems Journal*, 11, 65–84.

Briody, E. K. (2010). Handling Decision Paralysis on Organizational Partnerships, *CourseReader* (Internet Access), Detroit, MI: Gale.

Briody, E. K. (2013). Managing Conflict on Organizational Partnerships. In *A Companion to Organizational Anthropology*, D.D. Caulkins and A.T. Jordan, eds., Blackwell Publishing, Ltd., 236–256.

Briody, E. K., S. T. Cavusgil, and S. R. Miller. (2004). Turning Three Sides into a Delta at General Motors: Enhancing Partnership Integration on Corporate Ventures. *Long Range Planning*, 37, 421–434.

Briody, E. K., R. T. Trotter, II, and T. L. Meerwarth. (2010). *Transforming Culture: Creating and Sustaining a Better Manufacturing Organization*, New York, NY: Palgrave Macmillan.

Bundred, S. (2006). Solutions to Silos: Joining Up Knowledge. *Public Money and Management*, 26(2), 125–130.

Cash, J. I., M. J. Earl, and R. Morison. (2008). Teaming UP to Crack Innovation and Enterprise Integration. *Harvard Business Review*, November, 1–11.

Cilliers, F. and H. Greyvenstein. (2012). The Impact of Silo Mentality on Team Identify: An Organisational Case Study. *SA Journal of Industrial Psychology/SA Tydskrif vir Bedryfsielkunde*, 38(2), Art. #993, 1–9. http://dx.doi. org/10.4102/sajip.v38i2.993

Crossan, M. M. and M. Apaydin. (2010). A Multi-Dimensional Framework of Organizational Innovation: A Systematic Review of the Literature. *Journal of Management Studies*, 47(6), 1154–1151.

Curtis, J. R. and S. E. Shannon. (2006). Transcending the Silos: Toward an Interdisciplinary Approach to End-of-life Care in the ICU. *Intensive Care Medicine*, 32(15), 15–16.

Desjeux, D. and L. Zheng. (2002). The Itinerary Method: Comparing Intercultural Daily Life: The Case of Guangzhou, China. *Consumers, Commodities and Consumption: A Newsletter of the Consumer Studies Research Network*, 5(2). http://csrn.camden.rutgers.edu/newsletters/5-2/Desjeux.htm

Diamond, M. A., H. F. Stein and S. Allcorn. (2002). Organizational Silos: Horizontal Organizational Fragmentation. *Journal for the Psychoanalysis of Culture & Society*, 7(2), Fall, 280–296.

Diamond, M., S. Allcorn and H. Stein. (2004). The Surface of Organizational Boundaries: A View from Psychoanalytic Object Relations Theory. *Human Relations*, 37(1), 31–51.

Ferraro, G. P. and E. K. Briody. (2013). *The Cultural Dimension of Global Business* (7th ed.). Boston, MA: Pearson.

Foster, N. F. (2013). Designing Libraries in Liminal Space. Paper Presented at the American Anthropological Association Meetings, November 20–24, Chicago, IL.

Gulati, R. (2007). Silo Busting: How to Execute on the Promise of Customer Focus. *Harvard Business Review*, May, 1–9.

Herbert, C. P. (2005). Changing the Culture: Interprofessional Education for Collaborative Patient-centred Practice in Canada. *Journal of Interprofessional Care*, Supplement 1, May, 1–4.

Kirk, J. and M. L. Miller. (1986). *Reliability and Validity in Qualitative Research.* Beverly Hills, CA: SAGE.

Kleinbaum, A. M., T. E. Stuart and M. L. Tushman. (2008). Communication (and Coordination?) in a Modern, Complex Organization. Working Paper Number 09-004, July. http://hbswk.hbs.edu/item/5991.html, accessed on February 20, 2014.

Lencioni, P. (2006). *Silos, Politics and Turf Wars*, San Francisco, CA: Jossey-Bass.

Margalit, R., S. Thompson, C. Visovsky, J. Geske, D., Collier, T. Birk and P. Paulman. (2009). From Professional Silos to Interprofessional Education: Campuswide Focus on Quality of Care. *Quality Management in Health Care*, 18(3), 165–173.

Miller, L. C., B. B. Jones, R. S. Graves and M. C. Sievert. (2010). Merging Silos: Collaborating for Information Literacy. *Journal of Continuing Education in Nursing*, 41(6), 267–272.

National Institutes of Health. (2012). Overweight and Obesity Statistics. NIH Publication 04-4158. Bethesda, MD: Weight Control Information Network.

Neebe, A. W. (1987). An Improved Multiplier Adjustment Procedure for the Segregated Storage Problem. *Journal of the Operational Research Society*, 38(9), September, 815–825.

Newhouse, R. P. and B. Spring. (2010). Interdisciplinary Evidence-based Practice: Moving from Silos to Synergy. *Nursing Outlook*, 58(6), 309–317.

Rogers, E. M. (2003). *Diffusion of Innovations* (5th ed.). New York: Free Press.

Serrat, O. (2010). *Bridging Organizational Silos*. Washington, DC: Asian Development Bank, 1–5.

Shirey, M.R. (2006). On Intrapreneurship: From Silos to Collaboration. *Clinical Nurse Specialist*, 20(5), 229–232.

Thomas, J. A. and G. Hern. (2006). *The Organization and Architecture of Innovation: Managing the Flow of Technology*. Burlington, MA: Elsever.

Vermeulen, F., P. Puranam and R. Gulati. (2010). Change for Change's Sake. *Harvard Business Review*, June, 71–76.

Zorich, D. M., G. Waibel and R. Erway. (2008). *Beyond the Silos of the LAMs: Collaboration Among Libraries, Archives and Museums*. Dublin, OH: OCLC Research. www.oclc.org/research/publications/library/2008/2008-05.pdf

4 Collaboration for impact

Involving stakeholders in ethnographic research

Jennifer Watts-Englert, Margaret H. Szymanski, Patricia Wall, and Mary Ann Sprague

Introduction

Corporate research labs are on the decline. Economic hard times have caused corporate research headcount reductions and compelled researchers to look for external funding for their research agendas. According to Slywotzky (2009: 5th paragraph), "since the 1990s, labs dedicated to pure research – to the pursuit of scientific discovery – have seen funding slowly decline and their mission shift from open-ended problem solving to short-term commercial targets, from pure discovery to applied research." These increasing economic pressures are requiring corporate researchers to create and demonstrate a clear impact on corporate processes and offerings. At Xerox, we have found that our ethnographic research makes a bigger impact when we involve stakeholders in the research process.

Ethnography in corporate research, referred to as *Work Practice Study* within Xerox, was pioneered more than 30 years ago at Xerox PARC (now PARC, Inc.). Xerox founded Xerox PARC as a pure research laboratory with the goal of creating the Office of the Future; anthropologists were called in to enable *human-centered* innovation and design of technology and better ways of working. Lucy Suchman (1995, 2011) formalized the methodology at Xerox PARC by establishing the Work Practice and Technology group in 1989. Over the years, Xerox's ethnographic orientation proliferated to include ethnomethodology and conversation analysis, participatory design and visual co-design practices. Today four Xerox research centers – in California, New York, France and India – have work practice competency; all work towards the holistic understanding of people's activities in technology rich environments through the naturalistic observation, recording and analysis of these activities. Across the history of Work Practice within Xerox, our methods have evolved to engage the stakeholders of the research to greater degrees (see Figure 4.1).

Over the years, the focus of our work practice projects has moved from the critique and description of a particular setting's technology use and work practice to full engagement with the client to achieve organizational and service offering transformation. Along this work practice project

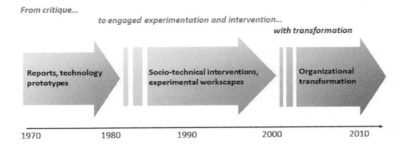

Figure 4.1 Progression of Xerox ethnography projects (de Kleer, Whalen, and Whalen 2004).

continuum, some projects have focused on, for example, the study of entire workscapes (Whalen and Whalen 2004), in airports (Suchman 1992, 1996), call centers (Whalen and Whalen 2011), mobile work (Watts-Englert *et al.* 2012), production printing (Sprague, Martin *et al.* 2007; Sprague, Woolfe *et al.* 2007; Colombino *et al.* 2011) and academic institutions (Wall *et al.* 2008). Other projects have involved the capture of the worker's knowledge and experience in socio-technical tools that helped facilitate better ways of working (Whalen and Bobrow 2011; Wall and Koomen 2011).

As stakeholders have become more involved in all stages of ethnographic research, this research has become more instrumental in transforming business and work practices (e.g. Kishimoto 2011; Plurkowski *et al.* 2011). This trend to directly involve stakeholders has created a radical shift in the way clients think about the utility of ethnographic methods. Whereas corporate ethnography was once only a research competency, it is now conceived of as a powerful tool to propagate organizational change, renovate a business culture and even add to an organization's external service offerings.

In order to create this kind of transformative impact, stakeholders must be closely involved in the ethnographic research. Through myriad techniques, ethnographers at Xerox have developed a dialogue between research and business groups – many from companies that have not historically invested in social science research – resulting in better uptake of study findings, customer-focused business initiatives and a rise in partnership opportunities with customers. While it can be challenging to maintain the rigor of ethnographic research when stakeholders become part of the research team, we have found that these challenges can be mitigated and that the benefits are worth the extra up-front investment.

What is a stakeholder?

Mirriam-Webster.com defines *stakeholder* as "one who is involved in, or is affected by a course of action." We consider anyone who might benefit from and/or act upon the findings of an ethnographic study to be a potential stakeholder. At Xerox, there are various levels of stakeholders who are invited to become involved in ethnographic research, ranging from research and business groups whose work could benefit from the findings of studies that have already been conducted, to business or research partners who commission an ethnographic study to answer specific research questions.

At one end of collaboration continuum are the *peripheral* stakeholders who could benefit from, or act upon, studies that have already been conducted (see Figure 4.2). These stakeholders could include research teams, corporate strategists or business groups whose work is related to the topics that have been studied in a past ethnographic project. For example, in the Xerox Future of Work study, peripheral stakeholders from the Xerox Information Management group were interested in using study findings to inform their strategy and the services they provided to Xerox workers (Watts-Perotti *et al.* 2009; Watts-Englert *et al.* 2011).

Peripheral-stakeholder collaborations usually begin with a session in which we share our study findings. We tailor our presentations to the peripheral-stakeholder audience by highlighting the findings that are most relevant to the work they do. In addition to presenting study findings, we may also conduct workshops with peripheral stakeholders to discuss the implications of the research for their work, and/or to translate study findings into solutions they could develop or offer. This kind of interaction is less collaborative because the peripheral stakeholders were not involved in the creation of the study questions and findings have been tailored post-hoc to highlight the most relevant information.

A second type of stakeholder is the *promoter* stakeholder: one who might not benefit directly from study findings but can influence the direction of commissioned research and/or how the research is used within the company. For example, managers who decide which projects get funded are important promoter stakeholders for ethnographic projects. In order to fund a project, they often have to champion it, justifying the cost and defending its value. In addition to funding projects, managers can also identify which groups might benefit from past or future ethnographic studies, and they can provide connections to the groups who might not otherwise be willing to listen to study findings. While promoter stakeholders may not benefit directly from a specific study, we still collaborate with them to define research topics and study questions, and to discuss implications of the research for the company.

Promoter stakeholders may also represent the organizations responsible for customer accounts and provide entree to study participants. In addition to gaining insights to their customers' practices, promoter stakeholders may look at an ethnographic project as a way to build a stronger relationship with the customers. This collaboration helps the promoter stakeholders better understand the kinds of work we do, and creates buy-in for making use of study findings and for funding future projects.

Promoter stakeholders are great assets in conducting an ethnographic study, especially when time in the client site is limited. These stakeholders can serve as important key contacts at the client site(s) who can participate in the project as a guide or liaison. This "trusted insider" is familiar with the people, culture and practices in an organization and can help with logistics, make introductions and, in some sense, authorize study participants' interactions with researchers. An example where a guide was an integral enabler of project success was for a field study of airline maintenance crews (Wall and Koomen 2011). In this project, a maintenance expert working at headquarters was identified as our "guide" for access to several maintenance sites during the course of the project. Since we required access to maintenance areas not normally accessible to the public, our promoter stakeholder negotiated access at each of five sites. It proved extremely helpful that he came up through the ranks of the maintenance organization as he had relationships with each of the sites and knew many members of the maintenance staff personally.

Partner stakeholders collaborate much more closely with us on ethnographic projects at Xerox. These stakeholders commission ethnographic studies, and become involved in all stages of the research. For example, a business or research group might request an ethnographic study about a specific topic or question that directly informs their work. In this type of partnership, we involve stakeholders in as much of the research as they are willing to participate in. Partner stakeholders provide input into study questions, accompany us into the field, participate in analysis sessions, work with us to determine implications of the findings for their work and help us share the findings with groups who might benefit from the study. We find that our collaborations with partner stakeholders can lead to the transformation of business and work practices because the partner stakeholder is invested in the research – not just financially, but personally as well. They help us tune the research questions and package the findings so they are relevant to the target audience. While we always expand our studies beyond the questions that our stakeholders ask, this tuning is a critical element that determines whether findings are taken up by teams who can act on them (Watts-Perotti *et al.* 2009).

Another stakeholder that we collaborate with is the *participant* stakeholder – the person who participates in our studies. When we conduct ethnographic studies, we always offer to present our findings back to participant stakeholders. Participants can benefit from findings by getting an outside perspective on their work, including their strengths and weaknesses. They can also help us refine study findings and help us brainstorm implications for new products and services that they might use.

Sometimes, the boundaries between these kinds of stakeholders become blurred. For example, a person might start out as a partner stakeholder, participating in all stages of a research project, and then become a champion, a promoter stakeholder. This happened in a production printing project (Sprague, Martin *et al.* 2007; Sprague, Woolfe *et al.* 2007), where a subject matter expert began working with our team as a partner stakeholder, and

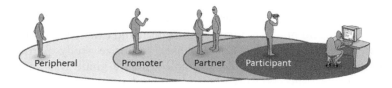

Figure 4.2 The four levels of stakeholders.

then became a promoter stakeholder when we began to present results to the technical community. During our presentations, he answered technical questions and vouched for the veracity of the findings, which were quite surprising to the technical community. His promotion of the findings of our study led to the creation of intellectual property, and convinced the company to create a new product offering.

When we work with internal Xerox teams, partner, promoter and peripheral stakeholders can influence the impact a project has within Xerox. Partner stakeholders, often representing services and/or technology interests, look to apply ethnography-inspired insights to inform corporate strategy and product or services innovation. Within the study site, participant and promoter stakeholders bring perspectives that can define what it takes to be successful within that organization as well as identify potential pitfalls the study is likely to encounter. Having stakeholders with different levels of organizational responsibility involved in the study, including management (senior and middle managers), business partners and participants, enables the researcher to develop a more comprehensive understanding of the work and the factors that influence it. This understanding is very useful to anticipate and mitigate potential risks associated with any recommendations resulting from a study. This was the case for a study of airline maintenance crews (Wall and Koomen 2011), where the focus of the study was airline, specifically maintenance crew, compliance in reading and acknowledging new maintenance advisories. Based on the work practice assessment, the team co-designed a solution to address the key issues that impacted those involved in the advisory workflow at every level (headquarters, management, supervisors, and maintenance crews). Understanding how the organization was structured guided the development of the technology and the plan for its rollout.

Ways of working with stakeholders

As more and more projects engage stakeholders outside the traditional C-level decision makers, methods for engaging them continue to emerge. Within Xerox, we have developed five key ways of working with our stakeholders, via (1) advisory board, (2) field visits with subject matter experts, (3) analytic data sessions, (4) co-design as an iterative research process, and (5) competency transfer. These are not mutually exclusive ways of engaging stakeholders. Instead, they are a guide, leaving open the specific combinatory use, which is always dependent upon the negotiated goals of the project.

Advisory board

When corporate research projects were standalone endeavors, it was not unusual for them to have advisory boards, an objective body to guide the development and execution of the project's strategy. As client partnerships have become the project norm, advisory boards can serve an even greater utility, playing a more active role in shaping the project's activities, even participating in the project's data collection, analysis and application of the findings. The heightened engagement of the advisory board has shifted their view from outside observers to looking from within. It is this involvement – advisory board as an open forum for collaborative projects – that we discuss here.

Watts-Englert utilized an advisory board to embark on a novel research project focused on informing the direction of Xerox's core business strategy. The Xerox Future of Work Project (Watts-Perotti *et al.* 2009, Watts-Englert *et al.* 2012) looked at the emerging trends on the cutting edge of work practice: mobility, distributed teamwork, communication, security, social media and paper use. This project was exploratory, and was not looking at the use of a specific product or technology, so the authors created an advisory board to anchor the research with practical business questions. Since the project did not fit the existing research mold, Watts-Englert strategically improved the odds for success by implementing an advisory board that would draw business group alliances into the project and promote the impact of the study's findings.

The goal of the advisory board was to garner visibility and support from relevant business groups and formalize a way to share project findings with these groups. Since the project's topic – the emerging trends of workers of the future – was of high interest and extremely timely, it attracted the attention of many in the organization. With membership open, the advisory board grew to more than 30 research and business group members, representing more than 14 groups/divisions across the company.

In partnering with the business groups, the researchers on the project encouraged product developers, business strategists and others to accompany the researchers into the field in order to see for themselves what the team was observing and documenting. While in the field, participant stakeholders were encouraged to help collect data and take ownership of their observations in the field, analyzing them and participating in project data sessions. By going out into the field, advisory board field-workers helped shape the research questions in unanticipated ways, and their exposure to the contingencies of fieldwork helped push these business group members' thinking out of their box. The result was more productive discussions about the findings. The advisory board field experience closed the gap between the work practice findings and their significance for solution design, so discussions could focus on deepening the analysis and moving design solutions forward.

The advisory board enabled members to connect with people they had not met before, and helped forge alliances that might not have been possible without the creation of this new community of interest. An outgrowth of the meetings and email group was a community website, a gathering place for interested people across the company to share relevant papers and ideas about the research being conducted. The synergies that developed as a result of this intergroup participation eventually led to the creation of new cross-company teams to facilitate these emerging collaborations.

Exposing business groups and product developers to fieldwork is a growing trend. Some organizations are engaging in consulting projects where senior management accompany ethnographers are sent into the field to learn about their customer population (see e.g. Schwarz 2011). Today's need for speed and development around fieldwork findings necessitates an efficient bridge. When corporate ethnographers are able to surrender some of their authority about fieldwork and data collection and invite their collaborators to accompany them into the field, a richer discussion around the implications of the findings can occur.

Field visits with subject matter experts

Many ethnographic studies involve different types of work, often in fields outside of the researcher's areas of expertise. Subject matter experts are both partners and participant stakeholders who provide relevant technical background information before going out into the field. Ethnographers gain background knowledge of the technology to be observed, making the observation more familiar and improving the quality of the observation and the questions. Providing background information to the ethnographers enforces the partnership between the team members, and helps the ethnographers to be fluent enough to understand the participants. The subject matter experts also contribute to the discussion guide containing the topics and range of questions to be investigated.

Subject matter experts played a strong role in a Xerox color digital printing project several years ago (Sprague *et al.* 2007). A study was proposed to understand how color matching of digital prints was achieved before a digital production print job was run. In order to proceed with the work practice study in print shops, the researchers prepared for the study by gaining more background on the technology they would be studying. Color experts within the department provided an introductory course on the technical details of color and color imaging. The course provided the researchers with a familiarity with the technology and terminology they would hear in the field. During this preparation, the color imaging experts were also provided guidance about what to expect in the field and how to behave and ask questions. Ethnographers, subject matter experts and the study's customers jointly developed a discussion guide containing the lead questions to be investigated during the study.

Once the team was prepared and the initial field sites were determined, the research team, consisting of two ethnographers and a color imaging specialist, went out into the field. One of the main goals was to better understand how print operators used the tools provided with the digital color printers to achieve a color match to the original provided for the print job. The assumed process was for the print operators to create a test print, make any adjustments needed to match the colors, reprint the test, and once the colors were acceptable to the operator, provide the test print to the customer for approval before running the entire print job.

The observed process was not as straightforward. In many cases, adjustments were made to the color printing device rather than the electronic file. In other cases, adjustments were made to the electronic file rather than disturb the calibrations and settings of the color printer. In the cases where the color printer was adjusted, the color imaging specialist noticed that the print operators used the provided tools in ways that did not match the specifications as laid out by the system designers. The design specifications of the machine assumed that incoming files would include an electronic color profile that would allow the machine to automatically adjust settings to provide an acceptable print. However, in reality, many files did not include electronic color profiles. Therefore, adjustments to these files were done by eye, meaning the operators used their own experiences, combined with a trial-and-error technique, to match the colors. Few, if any, measurements were available to allow the operator to "dial in" the corrections in a systematic method. Of particular interest to the color imaging specialist was how the color adjustments were done contrary to the specifications laid out by the color consortium on how color printing was supposed to work. This was a surprising insight to the color expert, and these random adjustments and unexpected uses of the tools provided were not isolated; this was observed at several sites during the study.

The observations of adjustments that didn't fit the expected model helped pave the way for a sweeping redesign of the tools that were provided for the color digital printer. These new tools made it easier for operators to make color adjustments by eye, when no electronic color profiles were available. Several patents were generated, leading to the development of new, more intuitive color matching tools. In the end, the user interfaces for several tools were also redesigned to make the information more usable for print operators.

There were several benefits from the insights seen first hand by our partner stakeholder – the color imaging expert. At first, the expert had not believed that the systematic color corrections were not being followed, but seeing the corrections as they were being done awakened him to the truth. His observations convinced him of the importance of going into the field to see how work was actually being done and led him to become a strong advocate of work practice, both in the color printing study and beyond. It also inspired his future research to help the governing body of color specialists to better understand how to make their specifications less confusing and more usable for the people actually using printing devices. When the study findings were presented to the customer and other divisions within the company, this partner stakeholder provided recommendations and support that added technical credibility to these striking findings. In this way the subject matter expert was not only a partner stakeholder but also became a promoter stakeholder, promoting not only the findings from the color printing study but also promoting ethnographic methodologies in future projects.

Analytic data sessions

Ethnography is an empirical method strongly tied to the data that one collects at a particular field site of interest. One of the most effective ways for engaging a group of disparate members around an ethnographic project is by bringing a piece of this field data for collaborative analysis in the form of a data session. Xerox has a long history of using these types of co-viewing data sessions to build community and shared understanding around research project findings (Suchman and Trigg 1991; Brun-Cottan and Wall 1995; Jordan and Henderson 1995). It is common for the data session host to bring analytic aids such as transcripts or schematics that help the participants to see or make sense of the data being analyzed. These analytic aids help participants point to what they are seeing in the data and foster a productive, grounded discussion.

Once the observations and interviews have been completed, involving the stakeholders in the analysis of the findings and subsequent discussions is another way of involving interested parties. Once preliminary findings are available, it can be useful to have a brainstorming session with stakeholders and other parties to gain outside perspectives on the findings and resulting implications. Stakeholders often know numerous contacts and implications related to the fieldwork findings that may not be readily apparent to the ethnographers, offering an expanded view of potential opportunities and resolutions.

Participating in these analytic data sessions regularly throughout a study builds up a capacity to see interesting interactional phenomena and patterns across data excerpts. As participants talk about what they are seeing in the data, it is important to continually ask for the empirical evidence for what they are observing by asking: How do you know this? What evidence do you have? Over time, participants from non-social science backgrounds begin to develop an ethnographic stance: an attitude that simultaneously honors data and theory by pulling in concepts and patterns and checking them against the data that have been collected.

Data sessions are valuable for fostering stakeholder relationships at all phases of the project. For example at the very beginning of a new project, recorded ethnographic observations can be used in a data session format to inspire promoter stakeholder brainstorming of possible project topics. Mid-project, data analysis sessions engage partner stakeholders in the discovery of the research process.

Co-design as an iterative research process

Ethnographic methods naturally lend themselves to collaboration, for in order to collect quality data in the field, trust and some degree of partnership with the participating members must be established. Co-design (Blomberg *et al.* 1993; Wall and Mosher 1994), the collaborative creation of a solution or technology with the target user group, is a process that grows out of the relationship that ethnographers establish with the participant stakeholders with whom they are working. In Xerox's iterative work practice methodology (see Figure 4.3), co-design begins with the first participant contact where it is communicated that no matter what type of project is at hand, the success of the project's outcome depends upon the relationship between the ethnographic researchers and the stakeholders who are involved.

Co-design workshops with participant and partner stakeholders can focus on process, technology, services and/or organizational improvements. Sessions with Xerox stakeholders can bring customer experiences into focus for the community of researchers, technologists and planners who are interested in developing technologies and services for those customers. Workshops to engage stakeholders in field data and the implications for business include: data sessions to share and discuss excerpts of video data, intellectual property workshops focused on field findings and their implications for developing patents, ideation workshops to develop technology and service concepts, advisory board working sessions to share field findings and implications for various stakeholder constituents.

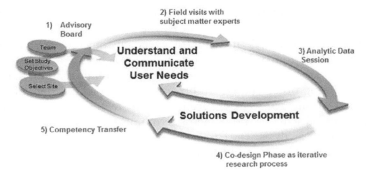

Figure 4.3 Xerox work practice methodology.

In partnering with the participant community in co-design, organizations are able to leverage and mobilize information from the people or environment in which the work is being accomplished. One project that translated ethnographic findings into a socio-technical system through a co-design process was the EUREKA Project (Whalen and Bobrow 2011). The project was originally focused on providing the Xerox customer service technicians with an online knowledge system (essentially the company's repair manual in digital form) to improve their repair of copier problems. Ethnographic observations revealed what the technicians really needed: a way to capture and share their own solutions to difficult, unknown, undocumented problems. So an expert system was co-designed around the technician work community; the technicians themselves would author and vet the solutions, so it would be "owned" by the work community itself. Co-design enabled the technicians' knowledge and expertise to be captured and shared by technology that scaled their everyday face-to-face practices.

In other co-design projects, the role of the workers can be "center stage" to the process. The Integrated Customer Service Project (Whalen and Whalen 2011) featured an experimental co-design process in which Xerox call agents, alongside Xerox researchers, created their own training program and a new learning environment. The project involved merging three different call-center jobs into one new job, enabling Xerox customers to dial a single 800-number to handle billing, supplies or service issues with their copier machine. In the co-design process, the workers themselves wrote a new training curriculum, based on their practical experience with a learning-by-doing instructional focus. Furthermore, the co-design team changed the call center's physical environment to create an open, work-group-centered environment that encouraged collaboration and sharing. Participation on the co-design team empowered the workers to take very active roles in making changes to improve their own performance and learning.

The way in which co-design plays out in any client partnership, and the degree to which the workers figure in the process, is particular to each client and their needs. In one retail copy shop project (Vinkhuyzen 2011), we combined the use of analytic data sessions and the co-design team to create a shared understanding with our client partner. The copy shop was having difficulty with its order taking; almost every customer order had to be redone or added to at pick-up because it had not been completed to the customer's specifications. To highlight the miscommunication that was happening during order taking, we brought videotaped excerpts of order-taking interactions to weekly meetings that featured thematic issues (e.g. upselling, discussing price, shop terminology, etc.), which we had discovered in our analysis. The employees on the co-design team (sometimes the ones in the video!) would share their expertise by commenting on the data and brainstorm better ways of delivering customer service in these contexts. From these co-design data sessions, we were able to develop an online training program in customer service skills that used video recordings of actual customer encounters as one of the key instructional materials.

Co-design processes are partnerships with stakeholders that are tailored to the needs of the project. Depending on the desired outcomes of these engagements, stakeholder participation on the co-design teams can be peripheral or be positioned center stage to the solution development. Either way, the key is to develop a team that includes stakeholders who are invested in the process and outcome of the project; these champions will pave the way for the success of any technology intervention or process implementation.

Competency transfer

Recently, some stakeholders have gone beyond a desire to benefit from ethnographic research to invest in creating an internal ethnographic competence. This has happened both inside Xerox and in a client organization. Through a process of competency transfer that involves classroom training and mentoring, employees within the stakeholder organization reach a level of proficiency in some ethnographic skills. Sometimes clients (both external and internal) request mentorship and learning workshops in addition to research on technology development or understanding customers. For example, a project for an external client on mobile telepresence (Isaacs *et al.* 2012) also involved the residency of a partner stakeholder to closely follow the research process. Recurrent requests to teach ethnographic field methods have resulted in the formalization of an ethnographic certificate program within Xerox.

One model for competency transfer mirrors more traditional learning trajectories including classroom and practical training phases with progression towards certification. Plurkowski *et al.* (2011) details an initiative to transfer work practice competency to subject matter experts in a Xerox business group that began to sell its services and solutions to clients outside of Xerox. The rationale for this stakeholder's investment in competency transfer was threefold. First, the organization had prior project successes that showed a work practice study could illuminate how the work is accomplished; these practices could be integrated into technologies, reducing production times and error rates. Second, they had made a commitment to strengthen the consulting methodology with a hybrid combination of normal process engineering methods and qualitative, employee-centered approaches such as the toolkit that work practice study provides. Third, whereas in the past the business group had asked research for help with their client engagements, they wanted to be able to singlehandedly provide end-to-end, integrated solutions themselves.

To transfer ethnographic competency to this internal Xerox business group, Xerox work practice analysts across three research centers developed training materials and workshops designed for professionals who were new to social science research, with the goal of creating a self-sustaining work

Table 4.1 Training levels of work practice (WP) competence.

Competence Level	Description
Awareness	"I can recognize an opportunity for WP value."
Introductory	"I can identify where to position WP as part of a solution."
Apprentice	"I am training in WP methods." Classroom Training (Level 1): "I am learning WP methods." Field Training (Level 2): "I am practicing WP skills in the field."
Xerox Certification	Certified Work Practice Analyst "I can effectively use work practice methods independently and can contribute to a WP project team." Expert Certification: Certified Work Practice Project Manager "I can design and lead a work practice study effort." Certified Work Practice Trainer "I can train others in Xerox WP (Levels 1–4)."

practice training program. The Awareness level work practice (WP) training (see Table 4.1) was designed to be 90 minutes or less in order to fit into the extremely busy schedules of Xerox salespeople, and eventually was transformed into an e-learning module that could be deployed easily over the web. The Introductory level begins the certification path; managers and prospective work practice analysts take this one-day course to develop an intuitive sense for where work practice could be fruitfully applied. At the Apprentice level, candidates engage in a week-long classroom training that features a work practice study involving all phases of the work practice methodology in a real client site. Subsequently, apprentices engage in one or more additional work practice studies with the guidance of a mentor until adequate proficiency in the methodology is reached.

Once certified, candidates are able to use work practice methods independently as an Analyst, or they may attain expert certification. The expert certifications acknowledge two roles: the Project Manager, who oversees the resources and activities of a work practice team throughout the study, and the Trainer, who is able to teach and mentor other candidates towards certification, making the center self-sustaining.

Another project that also resulted in a self-sustaining center, the Fujitsu Social Science Laboratory, employed a different model of competency transfer (Kishimoto 2011). In this case, researchers relocated to Tokyo to mentor and work alongside the stakeholder partner's employees. As PARC project lead Whalen (Kishimoto 2011: 327) says, the center "was achieved not by Fujitsu copying PARC's ways of doing applied ethnography but rather by adapting our principles to their own operation, to their own organization's culture." This involved 3 years of mentoring and incubation inside the organization. Today, Fujitsu is using ethnographic fieldwork as a service to help their customers innovate their businesses.

Teaching ethnography as a service is not without its challenges. The most difficult thing to impart on novice practitioners is the analytic expertise needed to be able to "see" what the field data is revealing (Jordan 2011). Transferring ethnographic research skills to business group stakeholders also raises a key tension among practicing corporate ethnographers: Should ethnography support technology-focused research or stand alone as the discovery science that it is (Whalen and Whalen 2004)? While this debate continues, we acknowledge that despite its challenges, of all the ways of working with stakeholders discussed here, competency transfer renders the strongest partnerships because of stakeholder's commitment and the time and investment required to achieve the transfer.

Managing stakeholder involvement

When involving stakeholders in the ethnographic research process, it is important to consider how their participation will impact the study. On the one hand, stakeholder participants could put an extra burden on ethnographers who must manage the presence of an additional person(s) and their behavior. On the other hand, stakeholder participants overwhelmingly turn out to be strong advocates for the research methodology, its findings and application(s). In the end, the benefits stakeholder participants bring to the research process outweighs any additional work, but here are some of our best practices for success.

In all situations, bringing people into the field with you is a concern because it can affect your rapport with customers and impact the way they interact with you. Whereas interviewing a participant alone sets up a manageable dyadic interaction, bringing along one or more stakeholders can create an uneasy two- or three-against-one dynamic, making the participant feel insecure about speaking freely. Moreover, if stakeholders do not feel comfortable going into the field, the uneasiness of the interaction is increased, further impacting the researcher's ability to gather data and build trust with the study participants. One way to effectively manage stakeholder participants is to introduce them to study participants early on in the project, so familiarity and trust can be established.

Since partner stakeholders may not have previous experience with ethnographic methods, it is important to provide an overview of the approach, training regarding observation and interviewing techniques, and to set expectations for their role in the field. If possible, ask them to take a role in the field activity, for example taking responsibility for audio recording, to make them an integral part of the team rather than a tag-a-long observer. Also, clarify expectations about interactions at the field site, for instance, if they are participating in an interview, clarify what the expectations are for introducing topics or questions so they do not inadvertently interrupt, or worse, derail, the flow of the interaction. You can also ask them to summarize their experience including their impressions, any surprises or insights, so they take the opportunity to reflect on the experience and contribute to the data analysis.

Another concern when involving stakeholders in the research process is their ability to learn how to conduct themselves as objective observers, and be open to learning about participants' work practices and points of view. It is not uncommon for stakeholders to jump to conclusions too early based on a small amount or a subset of the data, especially when they have a preconceived agenda they would like to reinforce. For example, some stakeholders may come to the field with their own ideas for what new features should be incorporated into a product, and they may attempt to confirm the validity of these concepts in the field, rather than being open to understanding the work practices of the participants. Furthermore, in an interview situation, stakeholders can unknowingly bias their interactions with participants by asking leading questions (e.g. "That process results in errors, doesn't it?" or "How would you like it if the product had this new feature in it?").

A great way to manage novice stakeholder participants is to give them guides for their expected field behavior; their performance aids can remind them of the appropriate stance they should take with study participants and give them a list of unbiased questions the study aims to answer. Workshops can be a constructive way to engage stakeholders with study data and encourage in-depth discussions around the emerging results and their implications for stakeholder interests. Organizing working sessions with stakeholders doesn't have to wait until data collection and analysis are complete. Interactions that take place early on in a study not only help stakeholders connect with the data; they can provide an opportunity for stakeholders to provide insights, add new questions to the study, verify or clarify findings, suggest new contacts for fieldwork and build trust with the research team.

Stakeholders who accompany researchers into the field prove to be valuable allies in the research process. Stakeholders bring their own expertise to the field, which may lead them to notice things that the ethnographers might miss. In addition, by participating in the research process, stakeholders can develop their own understanding and empathy with participants; to convey this in other ways would be much more time consuming and less successful. So, when considering the time invested in taking stakeholders to the field, consider the time saved in recruiting a knowledgeable champion for the findings of the current ethnographic study as well as potential future work.

Despite the extra work bringing stakeholders into the field may cause, it is still worthwhile for several reasons. Most importantly, stakeholders who have been brought into the field have repeatedly stated that it has given them an appreciation for ethnographic research and the value of its findings. This first-hand observation often helps stakeholders to better see the complexity of the work done by participants and the conditions that are worked under that may often change outcomes. It has often been seen that such on-site observation can help to validate the findings in ways that cannot be duplicated by reports or videos. When stakeholders buy into the research method and its findings, they are more likely to serve as champions for ethnographic projects in the future. Not only do stakeholders who have gone into the field use ethnographic findings more readily, they also share these findings with colleagues which can accelerate the adoption of organizational change.

Managing stakeholders is both about optimizing their participation with the study participants in the field and leveraging their role within the stakeholder organization. With a little preplanning, stakeholder participants can become savvy observers and interviewers that bring their own unique perspective to enhance the study's outcome. Once stakeholder participants have been in the field, they more readily communicate their experience with their organization and increase the chances that the study will have impact, especially if the study findings are packaged for distribution (e.g. podcast, brochure, power point, etc.).

Types of impacts resulting from collaboration with stakeholders

Collaborating with stakeholders can have significant impacts along a range of dimensions. Among the most obvious impacts are those captured in the form of new products, features, technologies or services. This was the case in a study with a university bookstore where a collaboration around the design of a system to create custom course packs resulted not only in improvements to the course-pack creation technology, but also identified a need for a copyright management system to automate the labor-intensive process of obtaining and tracking copyright permissions from publishers for course-pack materials. This system was developed and was added as a product offering.

In some instances, new ideas or improvements can be realized as intellectual property. This was the case in a study of production print environments, where observations of production print shop operators resulted in the design of an improved color-editing capability. Insights from the field illustrated operator struggles with a multi-layered color editing tool, as described above (Sprague *et al.* 2007). This led to an improved design embodied in a patent, which was implemented and incorporated in subsequent releases of the product software.

Collaborations with stakeholders can lead to new service offerings or expand existing lines of business. A new line of business at Xerox, which focused on student assessments for K–12 schools, grew from a research collaboration with local school districts, initially to explore teaching practices and opportunities to support teachers in achieving educational objectives (Sprague and Fuhrmann 2013). To date, this collaboration has resulted in the development of a product (Xerox Ignite Educator Support

System™) aimed at facilitating student assessments and personalized instruction in the classroom. This represents a new capability and market opportunity for Xerox.

Collaborations with stakeholders can uncover new market opportunities as well as influence strategy directions. The Future of Work project (Watts-Englert *et al.* 2011) explored socio-technical trends (e.g. alternative work settings, increasing mobility, a digital savvy workforce) and how work is changing. The project uncovered real-world practices and generated thought-provoking implications about paper-to-digital transitions and the future use of paper in business processes, topics that were incorporated into corporate strategy planning workshops. The project also identified a high potential new market – mobile workers. We studied that in-depth in partnership with a technology team, who decided to develop solutions for that market – in part inspired by the findings from the Future of Work project.

Ethnographic study findings also become woven into stakeholders' daily work. We've seen several instances where project findings embodied in slides and illustrations have been incorporated into stakeholder plans and presentations. Stakeholders have also helped convince other stakeholders to take action based on study findings. The color printing project described earlier is an example of this. An imaging scientist who accompanied us to the field became one of our strongest voices into the product development community, resulting in significant improvements embodied in subsequent product releases.

Concluding thoughts

Corporate research is evolving: Financial hard times require researchers to seek client partnerships for funding. Industry partners are also evolving to seek out and embrace research processes in new ways. Corporate ethnography, a methodology that naturally engages customers, has fared well in this corporate research evolution and several techniques have been used to strengthen these partnerships.

Within Xerox, several methods have been used to draw stakeholders into ethnographic research projects. Advisory boards enable peripheral stakeholders to shape the direction of the research and build momentum in the community for new ideas, technologies and change. Field visits with subject matter experts set up for a strong research partnership as these stakeholders not only often provide entrée to the field but also facilitate the dissemination of the study findings for impact. Analytic data sessions enable stakeholders to look across interdisciplinary boundaries and actually see their customers and identify opportunities for products and solution development. Co-design practices that engage stakeholders in an iterative research process make it possible to harness this stakeholder knowledge and expertise to create better solutions and improved ways of working; the process delivers impact that the stakeholders themselves "own." And businesses are investing in ethnographic competency transfer to bolster their internal capacity to deal with their clients' problems and to create new service offerings.

Xerox ethnographic research has embraced stakeholders by inviting them to participate in the collection and analysis of field data. Analytic data sessions, advisory boards as field alliances, field visits with subject matter experts, co-design, and competency transfer are five activities that enable researchers and stakeholders to develop a common understanding grounded in data. As a result, ethnographic research and business stakeholders are becoming more closely aligned and heightening the potential impact of their collaborative projects.

While it can be challenging to involve stakeholders in the research methodology, these challenges can be addressed. Ultimately it is worth the extra work to address these challenges, given the benefits of involving stakeholders in the research methodology. When stakeholders are involved, the research is more grounded, and has a greater potential to generate actionable study implications. Involved stakeholders can also increase the likelihood that study findings are incorporated into future products or services.

References

Blomberg, J., Giacomi, J., Mosher, A., & Swenton-Wall, P. (1993). Ethnographic field methods and their relation to design. In D. Schuler & A. Namioka (Eds.), *Participatory design: Perspectives on systems design* (pp. 123–156). Hillsdale, NJ: Lawrence Erlbaum Associates.

Brun-Cottan, F., & Wall, P. (1995). Using video to re-present the user. *Communications of the ACM, 38*(5), 61–71.

de Kleer, J., Whalen, M., & Whalen, J. (2004). *Leveraging the Social* (Unpublished internal report). PARC, Inc.

Colombino, T., O'Neill, J., Martin, D., Grasso, A., Wilamowski, J., Roulland, F., ... Watts-Perotti, J. (2011). Seeing the right colour: Technical and practical solutions to the problem of accurate colour reproduction in the digital print industry. In P. Szymanski (Ed.), *Making work visible: Ethnographically grounded case studies of work practice*. Cambridge: Cambridge University Press.

Isaacs, E., Szymanski, P., Yamauchi, Y., Glasnapp, J., & Iwamoto, K. (2012). *Integrating Local and Remote Worlds Through Channel Blending*, CSCW 2012, Seattle, WA.

Jordan, B. (2011). Transferring ethnographic competence: Personal reflections on the past and future of work practice analysis. In M. H. Szymanski and J. Whalen (Eds.), *Making work visible: Ethnographically grounded case studies of work practice* (pp. 344–358). New York: Cambridge University Press.

Jordan, B., & Henderson, A. (1995). Interaction analysis: Foundations and practice. *The Journal of the Learning Sciences, 4*(1), 39–103.

Kishimoto, K. (2011). Fujitsu learned ethnography from PARC: Establishing the social science center. In M. H. Szymanski and J. Whalen, J. (Eds.), *Making work visible: Ethnographically grounded case studies of work practice* (pp. 327–335). New York: Cambridge University Press.

Plurkowski, L., Szymanski, M. H., Wall, P., & Koomen, J. A. (2011). The work practice center of excellence. In M. H. Szymanski and J. Whalen, J. (Eds.), *Making work visible: Ethnographically grounded case studies of work practice* (pp. 336–343). New York: Cambridge University Press.

Schwarz, H. (2011). Ethnography as Executive Exposure – Spectacle or Higher Education? *Ethnographic Praxis in Industry Conference*, Boulder, CO, September 2011.

Slywotzky, A. (2009). Where Have You Gone, Bell Labs? *Bloomberg Business Week Magazine.* August 27, 2009, www.businessweek.com/magazine/content/09_36/b4145036681619.htm

Sprague, M. A., & Fuhrmann, M. (2013). *Ethnography Supports Changes to Student-Centered Instruction*, TQR 4th Annual Conference, Ft. Lauderdale, FL. www.nova.edu/ssss/QR/TQR2013/sprague_fuhrmann.pdf

Sprague, M. A., Martin, N., Wall, P., & Watts-Perotti, J. (2007). Giving Voice to Print Production Facility Workers: Representing Actual Work Practices in the Streamlining of a Labor Intensive Production Print Job. *Ethnographic Praxis in Industry Conference*, Keystone, CO.

Sprague, M. A., Woolfe, G., Watts-Perotti, J., Martin, D., Colombino, T., & O'Neill, J. (2007). Ethnographic Studies of Digital Prepress Color Workflows. *ISCC Annual Meeting*, Kansas City, MO, April 29–30.

Suchman, L. (1992). Technologies of Accountability: Of Lizards and Airplanes. In G. Button (Ed.), *Technology in Working Order: Studies of Work, Interaction and Technology* (pp. 113–126). London: Routledge.

Suchman, L. (1995). Making work visible. *Communications of the ACM, 38*(9), 56–64.

Suchman, L. (1996). Constituting shared workspaces. In Y. Engeström & D. Middleton (Eds.), *Cognition and Communication at Work* (pp. 35–60). Cambridge: Cambridge University Press.

Suchman, L. (2011). Work practice and technology: A retrospective. In M. H. Szymanski and J. Whalen (Eds.), *Making work visible: Ethnographically grounded case studies of work practice* (pp. 21–33). New York: Cambridge University Press.

Suchman, L. A., & Trigg, R. H. (1991). Understanding practice: Video as a medium for reflection and design. In J. Greenbaum & M. Kyng (Eds.), *Design at work: Cooperative design of computer systems* (pp. 65–90). Hillsdale, NJ: Erlbaum.

Vinkhuyzen, E. (2011). *Interactions at a Reprographics Store*. In M. H. Szymanski and J. Whalen (Eds.), *Making work visible: Ethnographically grounded case studies of work practice* (pp. 205–249). New York: Cambridge University Press.

Wall, P., & Koomen, J. A. (2011). Designing document solutions for airline maintenance advisories. In M. H. Szymanski & J. Whalen (Eds.), *Making work visible: Ethnographically grounded case studies of work practice* (pp. 285–298). New York: Cambridge University Press.

Wall, P., & Mosher, A. (1994). Representations of work: Bringing designers and users together. In *PDC'94: Proceedings of the Participatory Design Conference* (Palo Alto, CA), Computer Professionals for Social Responsibility, 87–98.

Wall, P., Brun-Cottan, F., & Dalal, B. (2008). Work Practice in Education, Unpublished manuscript.

Watts-Englert, J., Sprague, M. A., Wall, P., McCorkindale, C., Purvis, L., & McLaughlin, G. (2011). *Exploring documents and the future of work*. In M. H. Szymanski & J. Whalen (Eds.), *Making work visible: Ethnographically grounded case studies of work practice* (pp. 109–127). New York: Cambridge University Press.

Watts-Englert, J., Szymanski, M., Wall, P., Sprague, M. A. & Dalal, B. (2012). Back to the Future of Work: Informing Corporate Renewal. *Ethnographic Praxis in Industry Conference*, Savannah, GA.

Watts-Perotti, J., Sprague, M. A., Wall, P., & McCorkindale, C. (2009). Pushing new frontiers: Examining the future of paper and electronic documents. *Ethnographic Praxis in Industry Conference Proceedings*, Volume 2009, Issue 1, August 2009, Chicago, IL, 197–208.

Whalen, J., & Bobrow, D. G. (2011). Communal knowledge sharing: The eureka story. In M. H. Szymanski & J. Whalen (Eds.), *Making work visible: Ethnographically grounded case studies of work practice* (pp. 257–284). New York: Cambridge University Press.

Whalen, J., & Whalen, M. (2011). Integrated customer service: Re-inventing a workscape. In M. H. Szymanski & J. Whalen (Eds.), *Making work visible: Ethnographically grounded case studies of work practice* (pp. 181–204). New York: Cambridge University Press.

Whalen, M., & Whalen, J. (2004). Studying workscapes. In P. LeVine & R. Scollon (Eds.), *Discourse and technology: Multimodal discourse analysis* (pp. 208–229). Washington, DC: Georgetown University Press.

5 Collaborating across and beyond the corporation via design anthropology

Alice D. Peinado

Introduction

Consonant with a complex view of organisations, anchored in an anthropological approach, I contend that companies can no longer seek discrete solutions to wider business issues. Viable, long-term solutions can only come from complex understandings of company contexts where a variety of variables are looked at holistically rather than segmentally. This requires companies to collaborate across divisions but also to move beyond their traditional territory to pair up with companies specialising in other domains. While such arrangements are by no means new, they move away from the tendency of corporations to be self-sustaining, megalithic entities embracing and incorporating a variety of fields. It can also be argued that such entities, however, are far from operating holistically and that the approaches discussed here might also contribute to creating greater collaboration within corporations as well. Because of its holistic understanding of business contexts in general and problems in particular, anthropology can contribute to develop collaborative solutions for successful business propositions.

This chapter bases itself on research conducted for a series of consulting projects in design anthropology carried out primarily within the banking and insurance industry – but it also incorporates theoretical approaches proper to organisational theory, consumer behaviour and design. This is consonant with a holistic, contextualised and theoretically informed approach to problems proper to an anthropological perspective. The research itself focused primarily on senior citizens, with the aim to develop new insights for products and services targeting this population segment. However, while seniors were being interviewed in order to assess their needs, company processes were also being observed in order to identify how customer experience and satisfaction could be improved. Overall, a holistic image of customers' needs and the company's capabilities to address them emerged over and above the needs of seniors. This perspective went to enrich the design process so as to develop appropriate design solutions to discrete problems. Ultimately, however, the research findings raised more issues than the design process could answer and pointed to the inherent limitations in consulting activities framed within a design thinking approach. Transformational change can be enacted within organisations only when and where deep structural changes are adopted at the organisation's level beyond the solution of discrete, bounded problems. This requires questioning the existing organisational structure and redesigning organisational processes.

Discrete "glitches", what corporate clients often seek to correct or resolve, are often embedded in much larger systemic problems. By pointing to the complex interplay of variables underlying (in this particular case) the development and delivery of services, I embed the research and its findings, as well as the design process itself, within a wider frame of action. Solutions, I argue, cannot be one of a kind, discrete and bounded. Collaboration beyond the specific service touch-point where the "glitch" might be occurring emerges as a key variable to ensure customers' overall satisfaction. However, when working within or for organisations, anthropologists are often weighed down by the complex dynamics proper to the organisations they are working for, and are as a result unable to tackle the deeper issues confronting them. Indeed, few anthropologists can hope to be called on to help enact deep strategic changes at the organisational level. However, some design driven consultancies have developed ways to advise companies with respect to strategic decision making. Typically, they have moved beyond traditional design issues related to product or service development to incorporate a more vanguard view of design as strategic process. In so doing, they address issues proper to organisational management as a whole, and not simply product development or marketing. Such attempts prove that headway is being made to develop a more strategic role with respect to organisations and their transformations from a design perspective. This is consonant with a view of organisations as evolving organisms that adapt to wider economic and social changes. Given their understanding of complex cultural systems, anthropologists have much to contribute to how organisations can transform themselves in order to adapt to these new challenges.

Part I: Collaborating with whom and towards which goals?

The literature on collaboration focuses primarily on collaboration with respect to innovation, but seldom addresses collaboration to ensure coherence at the level of customer experience. In such contexts, collaboration can be a means to maximise resources and cut costs – and obtain diminishing economies of scope. Hansen and Nohria, for example, argue that multinational companies need to learn how to collaborate across units to "leverage dispersed resources" (Hansen and Nohria 2004: 21). They write that

> while multinationals in the past realized economies of scope principally
> by utilizing physical assets (such as distribution systems) and exploiting

a companywide brand, the new economies of scope are based on the ability of business units, subsidiaries and functional departments within the company to collaborate successfully by sharing knowledge and jointly developing new products and services.

(Ibid: 22)

Hansen and Nohria (2004) have identified four barriers to collaboration in multinational companies. These are typically framed in a human perspective and are:

1   Unwillingness to seek input and learn from others;
2   Inability to seek and find expertise;
3   Unwillingness to help; and
4   Inability to work together and transfer knowledge (Ibid: 24–26).

Within this type of framework, efforts towards increasing collaboration are focalised on developing interpersonal and communication skills, team building and knowledge sharing at the individual and group level. While such efforts can be localised, they can also spread across geographically distant units spanning the company's regional presence across the world. Typically, in such cases, collaboration is aimed at enhancing creativity and insights' sharing within the organisation, with the goal to improve the development of new products and services. As noted, such endeavours typically address innovation processes or operations and fail to extend to actual collaborations across units responsible for product and service delivery to the customers themselves. A discrete, segmented approach to how services are delivered sees customers confronted with specialised interlocutors unable to provide holistic answers. As companies maximise efficiency by cutting costs and subcontracting services, customers navigate between different entities and are confronted with partial when not dissonant discourses and practices. Such a segmentation of the customer's experience goes counter to the considerable efforts engaged by companies to create brand coherence and which are usually developed and enacted at the marketing level.

My qualitative research findings bearing on customer service in the banking and insurance industry show that the four barriers to collaboration identified by Hansen and Nohria (2004) might not be the most important ones involved in failure to deliver consistent and coherent service to customers. Observations of customers' touch-points across services' pathways in several studies have shown that these are not always established with coherency as a first imperative. Rather, the actual organisational setup of the company might be responsible for a lack of coherency in practices across the customer experience pathway, rather than individual unwillingness on the part of employees to collaborate. In such cases, employees cannot share best practices, learn from each other or transfer knowledge because institutional barriers exist making it either difficult or impossible to do so. Intra-unit and intra-company processes need to be designed to allow for collaboration, crossovers and sharing among employees. This requires redesigning the organisation itself and how services are allocated and delivered. Most important, it requires questioning who delivers the services and how the different entities involved communicate, collaborate and decide on common practices.

Questioning and transforming organisational practices, however, is far from easy. Indeed, the nature of knowledge generation and sharing within corporations has a long history. Argyris addressed similar issues with respect to communication within organisations in the 1990s (Argyris 1994). He argued early on that where organisational actors are only engaged in operationalising goals, plans and values rather than questioning them, strategic approaches only sustain the status quo rather than transform it (Smith 2013). Knowledge emerges from a real questioning of what we do and how we do it – with an eye to the deep complex variables that might determine our actions. Argyris reports that he spent years observing

> corporate leaders talking to subordinates at every level in order to find out what actually goes on in their companies and then help it to go on more effectively. What I observed is that the methods these executives use to tackle relatively simple problems actually prevent them from getting the kind of deep information, insightful behaviour and productive change they need to cope with the much more complex problem of organizational renewal.
>
> (Argyris 1994: 77)

Too often organisations don't question the reasons and motives behind their actions, hence only seek simple solutions to problems. Addressing the underlying reasons for problems is akin to opening "Pandora's box" (Ibid: 79). A motivation to skirt away from issues might be due to "individual defensive reasoning" (Ibid: 80). However, deep-seated "organisational defensive routines" exist that can also counter effective learning processes and action (Ibid). Extending on Argyris's argument, the author argues that such routines can be institutionalised and lead to effectively avoid any questioning of decisions at the strategic level. Organisational strategies that might be reasonably adapted to answer certain issues will not be tested or will be simply pushed "under the rug".

Pushing issues under the rug is never a valid solution. In today's fast evolving and competitive service industry, corporations need to be able to deliver superior service to their clients. However, it is no secret that customers today display a tendency for being less loyal to brands than in the past. It is often stated that the younger generations especially are less hesitant with respect to changing brands either to test them or to seek satisfaction elsewhere. This decrease in customer loyalty is partially due to the disbanding of all personal relationships tying customers to the brand in all but the most high-end ones. The depersonalisation of services naturally undermines brand loyalty based on long-term personal relationships. Concomitantly, customers reinvent their relationships to brands and adopt new trends with respect to their shopping habits. The new communication technologies make possible for customers to develop new ways of exchanging information about, assessing and even criticising a brand – over and above interacting with it. Often companies integrate these new technologies without understanding their scope as well as their implications for today's customers. Expectations have changed and brands must take notice of them to succeed. It is not simply a question of communicating about the brand, but of delivering the quality service it promises.

A recent Ernst & Young survey on consumer worldwide trends has detected five new approaches to consumer shopping habits (Ernst & Young 2012). Consumers are less brand-loyal, expect more from brands and seek personalised service. The survey notably "reveals the prevalence of the 'chameleon consumer', a constantly changing persona, who defies the confines of traditional market segmentation" (Ibid: 2). While consumers seek more leeway in their choice of experience, they nonetheless look for "the human touch" and "individualised service" (Ibid). They look for "personalised communication", are extremely well informed with respect to offers and prices, and "want to have a greater say in how they experience service" (Ibid). In other words, they are increasingly difficult to please and much less captive than in the past. For Ernst & Young this calls for five "implications for business":

- Engage in dialogue with the consumer;
- Make service personal;
- Provide an end-to-end brand experience;
- Deliver consistent multi-channel service; and
- Make consumers business partners (Ibid: 3).

Collaborating within and across companies to insure customers have access to pertinent and efficient services at all levels of the customer experience would seem to be a challenge today. However, it is exactly collaboration within and across companies that emerges as one way to create coherent service pathways for customers. This is particularly true in an age where, as noted above, companies are required to simultaneously engage in effective and meaningful dialogue with their customers but also deliver services across a variety of distinct channels.

Part II: Knowledge generation and anthropology's strategic potential

A design approach steeped in anthropological research might provide both insights and solutions to today's quandary regarding how companies might develop new ways to engage with actual and potential consumers. Engaging in a dialogue with costumers requires understanding the customer's point of view, seeing "the world as other people do" (Tripp 2013: 59). Personalising one's services entails adapting oneself to that worldview. Customer experience has largely to do with how customers interact with a company throughout the various service touch-points. Lee, Chung and Nam have recently argued that in order "to design a cohesive experience, all the touch-points should be integrated" through a coherent design strategy (Lee, Chung and Nam 2013: 15). However, according to these authors, only certain aspects of the *"servicescape"* can be designed, others, notably linked to the service staff's "interpersonal skills, empathy, attitude, and knowledge, are hardly designable" (Ibid). Organisations typically pay a lot of attention to the designable aspects of the various touch-points their customers have access to. These might include designing the physical and virtual space, the brand's identity, advertising or media access throughout the various stages of what has been defined as the *Brand Touchpoint Wheel*, that is the various physical and virtual sites through which customers' interact and engage with a brand. Lee, Chung and Nam rightly point out that these designable aspects do not address issues related to, for example, empathy. However, as Tripp argues, there is no service without empathy (Tripp 2013). Successful service entails understanding the customers' expectations. Tripp contends that some companies have begun to design with empathy in mind leading customers to develop intense brand loyalty. For Tripp, "the success of a service inherently depends on the person being served, not necessarily on corporate goals" (Ibid: 59). Ultimately, Tripp calls for "deep design research" so as to be able "to understand culture and identify the peculiar" (Ibid: 61).

Qualitative research of the kind conducted in design anthropology enables companies to identify and empathise with their customers' world – this is typically what anthropologists are good at. However, understanding consumers so that they might become one's customers and stay so is only one part of the equation. Tripp's call for deep design research, of the anthropological kind, does not tell us how to address the real issues of bringing about that empathic relationship. Typically, design consultancies might address this by talking about shared conceptual spaces between the brand and its customers and the value of storytelling to the detriment of actual interactions. However, companies need to understand how they do business. They need to see how their own management practices are in line with their brand identity and the experience associated with it. While understanding consumers can come relatively "easy", changing one's deep-seated ways of doing business might not. Yet, this is essential in order to create the empathy-based services these companies are aspiring to as current ways of doing business go counter to the establishment and delivery of such personalised services.

Typically, organisations fail to address the real problems related to dialogue and personalised service because of issues proper to the organisation's structural set up. These issues affect the end-to-end brand experience and hamper companies from seeing customers either as individuals or as business partners. While design solutions can help to establish meaningful brand-client relationships, real changes with respect to how consumers overall and customers in particular both perceive and experience specific services will only come through a re-hauling of deep-seated management practices beyond the service delivery level. This calls for organisational design anchored in an understanding of organisations as complex, interdependent systems. With their view of cultures as complex wholes, anthropologists are particularly well equipped at identifying and acting upon what might be in inadequacy with a company's goals with respect to customer service.

Anthropological research in and across corporate organisations has a long history (Cefkin 2009). However, as Fischer eloquently writes, corporate anthropology has to take an ethical stance with respect to the people it serves (Fischer 2009). This stance has as much to do with the responsibility anthropologists have, as consultants, to their clients, as it addresses the responsibility they face as anthropologists to bring value to their other constituencies. "If accountability to business needs and to professional charges are two audiences", Fischer states, "other audiences include the local workforces as well as the clients, customers, or users of the corporate services and products" (Ibid: 229). I call for an ethical standpoint in our professional practices by arguing that anthropologists can go beyond these constituencies by taking an organisation-based stance in their approach, in order to create value for both companies, their customers and society at large. Anthropologists practicing within or for the corporate world develop insights that often go beyond the brief with which they have been entrusted. Unlike their clients, they have difficulties circumscribing the field in which they carry out research to discrete, concrete problems because of a discipline-based tendency to look at issues within their embedded contexts via a holistic approach. As such, while they can definitely provide discrete understandings to bounded issues, their analysis often reaches beyond to an appreciation of these issues' linkages to wider contexts within and beyond the corporation. At best, clients are often not able to incorporate this knowledge, or deliberately choose to disregard it as impossible to integrate because of institutional barriers. However, answering to customers' needs and demands might require restructuring the way services are delivered, which in turn requires reviewing not simply work practices but also the way services are organised and the labour chain structured. Seen from this perspective, there can be no end to the cascading set of deep changes needed to actually fulfil a customer promise. These questions might not properly speaking address specific ethical issues, but they are ethical in that they bring to the fore the role of anthropologists as being, on the one hand, at the service of industry, and, on the other hand, as advocates for both customers and employees. It can also be argued that some of the issues addressed here have to do with the organisation of labour itself – with respect to the dematerialisation of services and delocalisation – and hence are ethical in essence.

Developing and articulating knowledge that both serves customers' needs and addresses clients' limitations – not to mention the workforce's organisation capacity to implement changes – is difficult to achieve. Where corporate clients are not looking at overhauling institutional barriers, solutions can only go so far. As a result, much of the knowledge generated through research goes lost. Worse still, the corporate or design anthropologist might decide not to share her insights because they are too challenging or disturbing. Part of the endeavour, therefore, consists in knowing how much to tell and what to keep out of the final presentation to the client without compromising the research's value. This is an exercise that is far from easy to accomplish, as it requires an understanding of the client's position and influence within the organisation, as well as good communications skills. Ultimately, it is a question of understanding how to bring about change within organisations.

Part III: Concrete practices and institutional hurdles

The qualitative research that I carried out within the banking and insurance sector revealed a number of problems related to how companies in this sector engage in and do business. The research was carried out over a period of approximately 5 years and involved altogether four consulting projects in design anthropology that focused on a variety of topics ranging from consumers' perception of bank and insurance companies to specific communication and service development practices in this sector. Several projects aimed at understanding the consumer habits of senior citizens. While this was not always systematically the case, given the focus of the research, in several instances the research pointed to the dysfunction of company practices due to a lack of communication and collaboration within companies generally, but in some specific cases also and more specifically because of conflicting practices across company divisions, subsidiaries and increasingly sub-contracting firms. The research consisted primarily of open-ended interviews with costumers and/or employees, observations in bank and insurance agencies and on telephone platforms. The research questions across projects varied, but overall they often were complementary and the information gathered incremental. Interviewees could be but more often than not were not exclusively senior citizens. The research was carried out exclusively in France.

When specifically researching costumers' experiences of specific services within the bank and insurance sector, I generally found that customers often complained about the overall quality of both bank and insurance services. Customers specifically complained that they were systematically confronted to discourses and practices that varied from one touch point to another of what was considered as one service. This was due to the fact that any given customer could subscribe to a service that, unawares to her, would systematically lead her to engage in business with several divisions of the company that were in some cases managed by subcontractors. For example, this could happen because the customer had wanted to subscribe to an initial loan through her bank establishment. At each stage, whether this consisted of the loan subscription, loan repayment or loan termination process, the customer was confronted with a set of different interlocutors via a variety of touch-points with often distinct if not contradictory discourses and practices. The research revealed that the customer did not understand why she had so many interlocutors beyond her initial counsellor, and why their discourse and practices changed. This led her to question the quality as well as the trustworthiness of the service. The customer often indicated that she would not engage herself with the same service again, precisely because of this incoherency in the overall service delivery process.

Observations of employees operating within the different touch-points of the loan service revealed that not only they depended from different company divisions, but also that these were increasingly subcontracted out to different companies. Typically, a different entity managed each stage of the loan process, with subcontractors often entrusted with those stages beyond the initial subscription of the loan. Consequently, employees operated within separate entities with different strategic goals. The discourse and practices they engaged in were adapted to the goals set out by the division (or subcontractor) in charge of that particular stage of the process and were not necessarily in adequacy with the company's, let alone the brand's overall promise. As a result, customers were not faced with a coherent, continuous offer and were at best lost navigating between the different entities or at worst frustrated if not angry. While the loan subscription could be initially lived as a positive experience, subsequently it often left customers weary and frustrated as to how the process was handled.

The customer experience was often fragmented, disjointed and lacking in coherence overall. In the case described here, the customer having subscribed to a loan through her banking establishment and wanting to repay it, subsequently discovered that the loaning institution was not the same as the one managing her banking services. Repaying the loan, something the customer might have thought as a relatively straightforward procedure, in reality involved a variety of steps rather complicated in practice. Whether trying to do so in person at her bank or going through her bank's Internet portal, the process involved a set of different legal entities that she usually would not interact with and which required her to engage in several different steps. Communication between these entities was not smooth, leading to contradictory information about the amount of money due, how to repay it and the delays involved for doing so – adding to the difficulty to repay the loan promptly. In this instance, brand coherence emerged as illusory as the customer navigated divergent worlds where not only the brand identity became progressively unclear, but also the very nature of the service she had subscribed to changed depending on her position on the customer's path.

Far from being uncommon, such differences in practices are often the result of deliberate strategies engaged in by organisations. In this specific case, experiencing difficulties in repaying one's loan might be due to the company's deliberately placing hurdles to the customer's doing so. Employees indicated to me on several occasions that it is not at all advantageous for the company to see one's client repay a loan ahead of time. As a result, such hurdles are there to discourage rather than encourage loan repayments over and above the established monthly repayment plan. This favours the company, but is perceived by the customer as discriminating and unfair – if not outright frustrating and contrary to the brand's promise of service. Organisations, therefore, are pulled in different directions depending on whose interests might be taken in consideration. It was clear from the research I carried out, that the marketing division did not have the same priorities as, for example, the loan repayment unit. Different players within the organisation have different agendas and all of these combined affect the customer's overall experience.

Predictably, the organisations studied were unable to address what were identified by the research as the more dysfunctional practices with respect to the overall services' coherency. The design process that in this specific case followed the research stage focused on a very limited and circumscribed set of solutions aimed at improving customer satisfaction at one of the service's touch-points rather than through the process as a whole. To be fair, the organisation's inability to address the problems that had been identified through the research was not due to any unwillingness on their part, but rather to the difficulties inherent in creating coherent customer pathways across divisions and beyond company boundaries. Typically, the anthropologists had been hired by one particular division to accomplish a specific task – often within the realm of R&D and/or marketing. With hindsight, the task could only be fully addressed by bringing other stakeholders in the organisation to the table. This was not (always) possible. Indeed, the research confirmed that while customers often have a monolithic notion of organisations, these are comprised of several entities with different functioning modalities and goals. Anthropologists, like the end consumer, are faced with the same complexity.

More disturbingly, the research showed that organisations might be unaware of the highly dysfunctional nature of their practices from the customer's perspective. This is due to a certain degree of opacity with respect to the different divisions' operations, or, in several cases, with respect to those of the subcontracting companies hired to deliver part or all the services. As noted above, it can also be a function of deliberate strategies put in place by different divisions and subcontracting entities with respect to their particular goals. While employees at the "floor" level are often alert to the incoherencies inherent in the services they are helping to manage, medium and upper level management across the organisation's various entities seem incapable of addressing these. With respect to upper level management, it can be argued that they are even contributing to their existence through their efforts to cut costs and rationalise the services' management process or maximise profits. Often a Tayloristic approach that maximises efficiency from the company's perspective modifies if not outright distorts the very service that it is meant to offer. Similarly, conflict of interests between the various entities delivering the services due to their own *raison d'être* might serve different units' interests to the detriment of the customers' ones or even the company as a whole.

By approaching companies from the vantage point of the customer – or the services' end users – it was possible to identify the rupture points in the customer experience. Thus, in the case evoked above, subscribing to a loan and repaying it is not managed by the same division – and indeed might even be subcontracted to another company. Information sharing across the various customer touch-points is not maximised. Similarly, practices differ leaving the customer not understanding why some particular action is possible at one level of the experience and not at another. Worse still, at each level of the experience the underlying motivations of the company might change. While the research focused on the bank and insurance sector, the findings can be easily generalised to other industries that have massively depersonalised and subcontracted their services in recent years. One case in point might be telecommunications providers. Customers navigate largely impersonal touch-points, attempting to find simple answers or have problems solved. Often, they feel impotent and frustrated – at best confused. The multichannel experience is fragmented, as each channel is managed as a separate entity even though it might be presented as a global package offer under a unique brand. It is clear that collaboration across divisions and beyond the company's boundaries could lead to better service.

Design anthropologists navigating all this often experience difficulties in having their voice heard. Typically, they engage in collaborations with specific individuals or, at best, units within organisations who are embedded in power relationship and have to manage different and often conflicting agendas. While one would expect organisations might want to generate knowledge about their practices and how to improve them, this is rarely the case. As Argyris noted, nobody wants to open "Pandora's box" (1994). The constraints within which one's clients within organisations operate are such that in the end the solutions that are ultimately accepted are often quite limited with respect to those originally envisaged. Throughout the design process, the actual users' voice is constantly being restrained and reformulated so as to fit the company's needs rather than the customers' ones. This is a reality little addressed in user-centred design approaches. Ultimately, this leads one to question to what extent users are really at the centre of the creative process. Indeed, what is often not enunciated clearly enough here is that "users" often refers to two categories of "clients" – the actual users of the product or services that one helps develop for the market and the various stakeholders within and around the organisation responsible for developing, producing and managing those products or services.

Conclusion

Discrete, specific solutions in the form of products and/or services targeting specific customers' segments, via a traditional market segmentation approach, do not really seem to work if companies are unwilling to address the five business points that Ernst & Young identified in their worldwide consumer survey (Ernst & Young 2012). They might represent single solutions but definitely cannot constitute breakthrough innovations leading to a truly satisfying costumer experience. In order to achieve this, companies should seek to implement holistic solutions that address clusters of problems – often requiring an overhaul of the way they do business. Unfortunately, companies are often ineffectual in developing let alone managing such solutions, because of a tendency to simplify problems and deal with discrete variables rather than complex issues. This is an issue proper to problem solving within organisations generally. Anthropologists, whether working for the corporate sector or with design companies, can provide the kind of knowledge needed to both analyse and increase a company's performance with respect to its custumers' needs and demands. This requires moving beyond an understanding of brand design as storytelling. While brands definitely tell stories, they are also constitutively engaged in creating customers' experiences. In many cases, designers have developed carefully constructed environments that develop a story sharing experience. Yet again, if actual everyday practices embedded in the divergent strategic goals of each of the units or subunits responsible for those experiences are not brought to converge and coalesce, customers will ultimately feel a disparity, a break in the brand promise to deliver a particular service. Today, customers are too savvy for companies to pretend they can effect change without transforming their business practices.

References

Argyris, C. (1994). Good communication that blocks learning. *Harvard Business Review*, July-August, 77–85.

Cefkin, M. (ed.) (2009). *Ethnography and the Corporate Encounter: Reflections on Research in and out of Corporations*. New York: Berghahn Books.

Ernst & Young (2012). *This Time It's Personal: From Consumer to Co-Creator*. London: Ernst & Young.

Fischer, M. (2009). Emergent forms of life in corporate arenas. In M. Cefkin (Ed.), *Ethnography and the Corporate Encounter: Reflections on Research in and out of Corporations* (pp. 227–238). New York: Berghahn Books.

Hansen, M. T., & Nohria, N. (2004). How to build collaborative advantage. *MIT Sloan Management Review*, 46(1), 21–30.

Lee, K., Chung, K., & Nam, K. (2013). Orchestrating designable touchpoints for service businesses. *Design Management Institute Review*, 24(3), 14–21.

Smith, M. K. (2013). Chris Argyris: Theories of action, double-loop learning and organizational learning. In *The Encyclopedia of Informal Education*. http://infed.

org/mobi/chris-argyris-theories-of-actiondouble-loop-learning-and-organi
zational-learning

Tripp, C. (2013). No empathy, no service. *Design Management Institute Review*,
24(3), 58–65.

6 Collaborating in visual consumer research

Russell Belk

Introduction

The saturation of visual representations in our lives has never been greater. As Jonathan Schroeder (2002) notes, "We live in a visual information culture.... [At] no other time in history has there been such an explosion of visual images" (p. 3). Raised with a background of television, the Internet, video games, PowerPoint presentations, YouTube, Facebook, multi-platform movies and TV episodes, and ubiquitous smartphone-captured photos and videos, the current generation of "born digital" consumers have come to expect visual images and quickly become bored with purely textual information. Stephens (1998) argues that sometime during the last third of the twentieth century images began to dominate words in terms of their power to capture and hold our attention. He explains the attraction of video in terms of its versatility, engaging techniques, and ability to provide more information in a time of shrinking attention spans:

> Moving images use our senses more effectively than do black lines of type stacked on white pages. In a video there is so much more to see, not to mention hear. Moving images can cut in, cut away, dance around, superimpose, switch tone, or otherwise change perspective.
>
> (Stephens 1998, p. xi)

Pink (2007, 2011b) adds that collaboratively produced images can also yield a multisensory sense of movement and place. But it is not only the power of video that is driving the shift from text to video, it is also increasing demand from clients, students, and consumers (Belk and Kozinets 2005; Kozinets and Belk 2006), to the extent that Sunderland and Denny (2007) once worried that videotaping was becoming synonymous with "doing ethnography." However, times have changed, and Patti Sunderland observes that "now in 2014, salient issues include online ethnography, photos on mobile phone ethnography, webnography, netnography, and ethnography being left in the dust in the era of Big Data" (personal correspondence). My perspective is somewhat different; despite the explosion of scanner data, the sophistication of web analytics, and the power of Big Data, their sterility and distance from the consumer creates an even greater need for penetrating ethnographic analysis and use of visual data.

During approximately the same time frame as the rise of the image – the last third of the twentieth century – there arose a crisis of representation that Clifford (1988) called the "breakup of ethnographic authority in twentieth-century social anthropology" (p. 22). He went on to conclude that "the West can no longer present itself as the unique purveyor of generalized ethnography... . With expanded communication and intercultural influence, people interpret others, and themselves, in a bewildering array of idioms" (p. 22) and called for continued experiments in ethnographic representation to try to overcome neo-colonialist power imbalances in the ethnographic project (see also Clifford and Marcus 1986; Lassiter 2005; Marcus and Fisher 1986; Ruby 2000). One result has been collaborative "paraethnographies" (Holmes and Marcus 2006, 2008; Marcus 2012; Mills and Ratcliffe 2012). Other experimental outcomes include critical ethnographies to empower the disempowered (Fortun 2012), reflexive ethnographies that critique the role of the researcher (Malefyt 2009; Marcus 2012), and distancing techniques, such as "observing the observers observing" (Marcus 2012). As Fortun (2012) explains, doing collaborative ethnography is not the same as fully democratizing the research process:

> The goal is not to give everyone a chance to speak, as a matter of fairness. The model is not the town hall meeting or the talk show. But it is about being open to intervention and foreigners, about hospitality, and solicitude. The goal is to come together – to literally collaborate, performing the labor of difference, to articulate something that could not be said, could not be brought together before.
>
> (p. 453)

Pink (2001, p. 44) notes that this sometimes empowers informants to challenge existing power structures, although this isn't necessarily the outcome. Pink further emphasizes that collaborative research should not be construed as being about giving something back in that this implies "hit and run" ethnography rather than making the informant more properly a participant in a joint research process.

Another of the continuing experiments is the move toward collaborative image making. As MacDougal (1991) describes this shift in perspectives within visual anthropology:

> About twenty years ago anthropologists and ethnographic filmmakers began to feel uneasy about the unchallenged dominance of the author's voice in ethnographic descriptions. Both began to open their work more fully to the voices of their indigenous subjects. The intervening years have seen a tendency towards dialogic and polyphonic construction in

ethnography.... . If we keep writing anthropology or making films today, we do so with greater awareness of the politics and ethics of representation.

(p. 2)

It should be noted that not all videographers, photographers, and visual ethnographers have been equally impacted by such calls for empowering informants through collaborative image making (e.g., see Burnett 2004; Emmison and Smith 2000; Gardner and Östör 2001; Heider 1997; Jackson and Ives 1996; Schirato and Webb 2004). At the other end of the continuum from collaborative image making is the auteurial school which holds that all images are theatrical and that there is nothing wrong with the director staging action and creating specific meanings (e.g., Braester 2011). There are also advocacy films and photo collections which are also dominated by the vision of the image maker. For example, Jacob Riis's (1890/1986) powerful *How the Other Half Lives* calls for action to improve living conditions in New York City slums (Jensen 2004); Dorothea Lange's (1981; Hagen 1985) photos of America's Great Depression, Robert Flaherty's (1922) *Nanook of the North* (Rabiger 2009), and Agee and Evans' (1941) *Let Us Now Praise Famous Men* all staged shots for greater impact.

I would not insist that all ethnographic image making must be naturalistic and collaborative. And naturalistic collaborative image making is not without its own problems. But in this chapter I look at some of the benefits of collaborative images, give examples of when they have been successfully employed in consumer research, and discuss some of the problems to be overcome in using this approach. I also try to expand the scope of what we mean by collaborative visual consumer research, especially within the framework of our digital age. For digital empowerment greatly changes the situation and does much to mitigate the concerns of the crisis of representation.

The changing scope of collaborative visual consumer research

There are many types of collaboration in visual consumer research, yet all remain the exception rather than the rule. In 2001, shortly after the September 11th attack on the Twin Trade Towers in New York, Rob Kozinets and I initiated a film festival at the annual conference of the Association for Consumer Research. We co-chaired it for 10 years before passing it on to other very capable hands. During that time more than 100 films aired at the festival. Only a handful involved collaborative research. Those that did either negotiated with those represented what would be included, showed the film to those portrayed in order to get their approval, or included clips shot by those portrayed in the film. For example, a film by Robert Aitken and Adriana Campelo entitled *Distant Voices* had indigenous inhabitants of an island in New Zealand create videos of what the land means to them. The editors compiled these videos, organized them, and let the voices of the inhabitants speak to one another and to the film's audience. A further step would have been to have involved the island inhabitants in conceptualizing and editing the video or helping them become independent in order to make their own films. Nevertheless, within the ACR Film Festival catalogue (some of which is archived at http://vimeo.com/groups/136972), this film is exemplary of the best practices of collaborative research.

In commercial consumer research, however, Sunderland and Denny (2007) often give the camcorder to the participants in order to get a more candid and personal point of view (POV) in their corporate research. For example, they have given small camcorders to college students going out for an evening of drinking and learned that those selected make it a policy to drink the "good" beers first, while they can still appreciate their taste and drink the less expensive beers later in the evening when they have already had a few and are less able to appreciate the difference. Since the researcher would be a "fifth wheel" in this context, this is not so much a moral effort to empower the participants as it is a practical effort to get better and more naturalistic data. It also allows the clients to feel that they get a richer picture of consumption practices by watching the resulting edited video. I also found that in studying the new black elite in Zimbabwe, that the best way to get them to feel truly comfortable in front of the camera in a postcolonial environment was to have pairs of other new black elites who were younger than them conducting and filming the interviews (Belk 2000).

A related method of visual collaboration in consumer research is to give the participants the (still) camera. Kelly Tian and I (Tian and Belk 2005), for example, wanted to study the meaning of personal possessions in a workplace. We gave employees of a high-tech firm disposable cameras and instructions to photograph the 12 most meaningful possessions in their office, cubicle, or area. After developing the photos we used them to "auto drive" (Heisley and Levy 1991) or visually elicit comments during interviews conducted at an off-site restaurant. This method has several advantages: It vividly brings absent objects into the discussion at a place where workmates cannot overhear; it typically elicits much richer data than unaided discussion; and it is often a more comfortable interaction because both interviewer and interviewee are looking at the photos instead of looking at each other. Furthermore, as Pink (2001) notes, "Ethnographer and informant will be able to discuss their different understandings of images, thus collaborating to determine each other's views" (p. 68). And we were subsequently able to reproduce some of the photographs in the resulting journal article analyzing the "extended self in the workplace" so that readers/viewers could better appreciate the objects and context to which the paper's text refers. Visual elicitation can also be done with visual materials other than photographs, including drawings, video, audio recordings, collages, and the natural environment (Drew and Guillemin 2014; Guillemin and Drew 2010, Pink 2011a; Pink, Hubbard, O'Neill, and Radley 2010).

As is evident with the use of disposable film cameras in the study of office possessions, that study used old-school technology (Murthy 2008). Today it would be more feasible and expedient to have people use their smart phones and e-mail the photos to the researchers (Lapenta 2011), or we could sample various times of day by calling or messaging informants to photograph what they are doing at that moment. Another example of old-school visual technology that can be updated is having informants physically construct visual collages. When colleagues and I studied consumer desire in the U.S., Turkey, and Denmark (Belk, Ger, and Askegaard 2003), we had participants in each country cut images from magazines and paste them on posterboard. They were to represent "desire" in these collages and after completion we had them discuss their compositions and choices of images. This was a very rich projective elicitation exercise which again resulted in reproducing some of these images in the journal in which our work was published (with color versions on their online website). But today it is more effective to have participants do collages by dragging, dropping, tilting, and resizing images and words in a program like the collage feature of Google's Picasa. A commercial counterpart is the eCollage™ of Buzzback. While in the desire study we had trouble providing participants in three different locations similar source material by using digital images it is easy to share the same set of images with everyone. Using a laptop or tablet computer works very well for such tasks and informants find these collages fun and easy to do.

Likewise, rather than take on the paternalistic task of teaching participants to make their own photos and videos with smart phones (e.g., Vicente, Reis, and Santos 2009; Wesolowski and Eagle 2012) and inexpensive digital cameras and camcorders, as well web pages and video blogs (vlogs), or to use photo upload sites like Flickr, and video upload sites like YouTube, we found that people in communities in a variety of world locations are already doing so on their own. Collaborations between patients and ethnographers have proved valuable for producing video diaries about cystic fibrosis and asthma. In other cases like Etsy, iCraft, and ezebee, they are also using similar sites to sell their arts and crafts. Patti Sunderland (personal correspondence) notes that

> commercial ethnographic research (including that of Practica Group) has – out of interest and necessity – moved into offering online ethnographic research, which can be powerfully visual in that participants use their webcams as a forum to both talk about and show their worlds; photographs and visual images (drawn from elsewhere on the web) are posted by participants and discussed; videos of experiences when away from webcams are also uploaded. In practice, online ethnographic research panels are highly visual mediums.

Malefyt (2009) and Suchman (2007) also point to the increasing use of visual collaborative online research in commercial ethnography.

On a grand scale, projects like "Life in a Day" demonstrate what can be done with global collaboration (e.g., https://www.youtube.com/

watch?v=JaFVr_cJJIY). The opportunity for research using such naturally occurring visual and verbal material is enormous. Techniques of "netnography" are still emerging and keeping pace with changing technologies and applications (e.g., Best and Krueger 2002; Johns, Chen, and Hall 2004; Kozinets 2010). Ethnographic research has also been conducted in online virtual worlds (e.g., Boellstorf 2008; Martin 2008), Massively Multiple Online Role Playing Games (MMORPGs) (e.g., Corneilussen and Rettberg 2008; Pearce and Artemesia 2009), blogs (e.g., Dean 2010; Rettberg 1988; Serfaty 2004), YouTube (e.g., Burgess and Green 2009; Pace 2012; Strangelove 2010; Wesch 2008), and Facebook (e.g., Drenton 2012; Miller 2011). Many of these important sources of self-presentation are automatically archived through sources like the Way Back Machine, while others are being archived by various secondary archivers. For example, the U.S. Library of Congress has been archiving all public Twitter messages tweeted since the start of this social medium in 2006. By October 2012, it was archiving more than half a billion tweets each day (Allen 2013).

Just what may be analyzed through such archives is open to the imagination. For example, a recent analysis of YouTube videos found that men were twice as likely as women to be the subject of stigmatization due to fatness, while men were 10 times as likely as women to be the ones doing the stigmatizing and ridiculing (Hussin, Frazier, and Thompson 2011). Drenton (2012) found that a group of teenage girls uploading an average of over 150 photos a month each to Facebook, used posting on each other's walls and tagging others in their uploaded photos to help "co-construct" their individual and aggregate senses of self. For example, a group of three girls were in a clothing shop dressing room trying on sequin-covered dresses. One girl snapped a joint photo of them in the dressing room mirror and instantly uploaded it to Facebook. Before they even left the dressing room others were posting back messages like "Cute dress! You should get it." In other cases, one of them would post a self-disparaging message on their photo, like "I really look terrible here," prompting others to post reinforcing messages like "You look hot! I wish I looked that good on a bad day" (Belk 2013). Because these messages look like uninvited endorsements, they enhance self-image without seeming narcissistic. LinkedIn is used in a similar fashion with specific skill endorsements from others, often followed by reciprocal endorsements of the endorser by the original target person.

Another naturally occurring form of empowered visual expression is found in some forms of urban graffiti or street art (Alvelos 2004; Emmanuel 2007; Visconti *et al.* 2010). As a sign of resistance, such visual graffiti differ in nature from gangs tagging boundaries of their claimed urban territories, although aesthetic expression in street art can itself be a form of resistance to urban banality (Banksy 2006, 2010). Resistance has a long history ranging from disaffected urban youth to disenfranchised indigenous groups (David and Wilson 2002; Ferrell 1995). Hocking's (2012) study of murals and graffiti in Belfast show how graffiti of religious protest have changed to murals for peace, only to be defaced with further graffiti of protest.

Analyzing new media self-representation

Full self-presentation is the norm in blogs, personal web pages, and social media. In such cases the role of the anthropologist changes from visual interpreter of consumer culture to interpreter of consumers' visual culture. In analyzing informant-produced self-representations we first need to consider what makes digitally mediated images and artifacts different from their analogue counterparts (Belk 2013; Lister 1995; Shove *et al.* 2007). The vast proliferation of such representations shows that digital images and films are quite easy to make and post online. In so doing, what were once private home photo albums (Chalfen 1987, 1998; Hirsch 1981; King 1984) or the personal archives of commercial photographers (Lesy 1973; Pinney 1997) are transformed into posted photographs for "friends" or the general public to see. Nevertheless, some of the same biases occur and the photos posted are likely to show happy people on celebratory occasions with new possessions (Belk 2010; Belk and Yeh 2011). However, whereas in analogue photography the photographer was seldom in the photo (Mendelson and Papacharissi 2011), with the advent of camera phones and arm's length "selfies," it has become normal for the photographer to appear in digital photos.

Like home mode photography, home mode films and videos have also become a valuable means of unobtrusively acquiring movie footage of home life (e.g., Chalfen 1988; Izhizuka and Zimmermann 2008; Rook 1985). The same advantages and biases that apply to home mode photography also apply to home movies. Contemporary archives of such films are found on YouTube and Vimeo as previously noted, along with a number of other film genres. But they do not contain the majority of older (or even current) home films and compiling an archive of footage in their many different historical formats remains a challenge.

With the tendency to "share" photos online via social media, it also becomes increasingly difficult for users to segregate different audiences for these representations (Belk forthcoming; John 2012). Children are often embarrassed if their friends see posts from their families and may get in trouble if their families see posts from their friends (Odom, Zimmerman, and Forlizzi 2011). When images are posted instead on an open blog or website, the audience is potentially anyone. While filters of social desirability and flattering self-portrayal are also evident in these cases, the online disinhibition effect (Suler 2004) and the desire to gain a large number of viewers and "followers" (Belk 2013), means that there is a tendency to admit foibles and faux pas in what sometimes becomes a "confessional" mode (Belk 2013; Holliday 2007; Renov 1996). Nevertheless, some of the photographer's or videographer's biases and intent seem to operate beneath their awareness but are evident in the images they post. For example, Nguyen and Belk (2007) found that veterans of America's Vietnam War photographed smiling American subjects in dominant positions with heroic upward camera angles, and fearful Vietnamese subjects in submissive positions with infantalizing downward camera angles. Another good example of analyzing photo biases is the analysis of *National Geographic* portrayals of subaltern consumers by Lutz and Collins (1993). These are just the sorts of power imbalances that collaborative ethnography is intended to redress.

With the shift to self-representation in digital online photography and videography, we should also be aware that our empowered inadvertent informants are telling stories about themselves (Furlong 1995; Walker 1995). Just as we ethnographers tell different sorts of stories through our ethnographies (Cayla and Arnould 2013; Cayla, Beers, and Arnould 2014; Van Maanen 1988), so do the collaborators. These range from confessional tales as noted above, to realist tales (especially in the travel genre emphasizing "I was there"), to impressionist tales of a more artistic nature. Although traditionally narrative analysis focuses primarily on text (e.g., Bruner 2002; Elliott 2005; Riessman 1993), recent treatments have begun to consider the unique features of visual narratives (e.g., Keats 2009; Page 2005; Pimenta and Poovaiha 2010; Riessman 2008). Given the easier possibilities of altering digital photos, we need to be more cautious not to believe everything we see. Through what Barthes (1977) terms *mythology*, there is often a deeper level of implicit meaning in an image than that of language or its literal meanings. For example, in advertising, implausible claims that using a product will make you attractive, beautiful, and admired cannot legally be made explicitly in language. But they can be implied by choice of the actors, actions, and *mise en scène*. Such semiotic properties of images require a more careful narrative analysis than words, which operate primarily at the level of language.

Issues in visual collaboration and new media

In specifically visual collaborations in print, online, and visual outlets additional issues arise in safeguarding informant identity since their image and perhaps their voice are a part of the research output. Besides the usual moral concerns about giving textual "voice" to informants, when the research is partly or wholly visual there are added concerns because of the difficulty of disguising participants' images and voices. These are concerns that do not occur in textual representation where pseudonyms may suffice to provide anonymity. And although editors of photos and videos may pixelate or blur faces and alter voices, this takes away a key benefit of visual media in helping the audience to put a human "face" to informants. Collaboration does not necessarily solve these problems, but puts issues of representation more fully in the hands of the collaborators.

Locations are also often difficult to disguise. There is also the need to negotiate what may be shown with collaborators, including what may be shown to whom and under what conditions. These issues become especially contentious when harm may potentially befall research participants if they are seen by certain others saying or doing the things that are included in an audio-visual research output. For example, Rana Sobh and I have done several visual research projects in Qatar and United Arab Emirates that were threatening both because of our desire to show images of covered Arab women outside of their *mahrem* (the circle of family who may gaze upon a woman) and our need to reveal negative attitudes that certain non-citizen residents hold toward the privileges of the dominant culture citizens and their rulers. The former images could bring shame on a family, while the latter critiques could result in informant expulsion from the countries of their birth where the research took place.

In the case of images of the *abaya* (gown) and *shayla* (headscarf) coverings, we agreed only to show these outfits if they were modelled by a non-citizen resident or on a mannequin. Because different Muslim cultures have different cultural understandings of proper Muslim female dress, guest workers such as maids were less conflicted about such modelling. In a related research project we were able to show female informants only when they wore a full facial covering (burka) in addition to an abaya and shayla. And in the case of the critical comments about local citizens and rulers, we agreed to get permission each time we wanted to show the resulting video to a specific professional audience and not to post the video to the web. These were workable compromises, but they did result in less transparent and visually engaging research outputs than is usually expected in visual research (see Sobh and Belk 2011a, 2011b, 2011c; forthcoming). But without collaboration, these projects would not have been possible at all.

Collaborative research can also be more difficult when the researcher and informants live in distant places and budgets constrain repeat visits. For example Joyce Yeh and I studied tourist photography by North American tourists in a variety of Asian, Antarctic, African, and Polynesian locations. As a part of this project I obtained the consent of one group of North American tourists to follow and videotape them as they toured Vietnam and Cambodia. My involvement during the tour was primarily that of participant observer and my camcorder was relatively invisible among normal tourist photography and videography being done at these sites. When I returned to North America I had informants e-mail me their trip photos and I interviewed them about their subsequent uses of these images. However, I could not afford to go to their various scattered locations to record these interviews. Instead, I transcribed the interviews and hired actors to enact their lines verbatim. As a result the resulting video and paper use these re-enactments, but the video is much heavier in voice-over interpretation than would have ideally been the case (Belk and Yeh 2011). Today capturing a Skype video interview could help overcome these problems.

Even though visual image making has become ubiquitous, there is also an issue of people "acting" when they know that they are being photographed or filmed. Sunderland and Denny (2007) do not find this to be much of a problem:

> From our point of view, the performance of routines – including those associated with the act of movie-making – do not in any way impede possibilities of cultural analysis. To consider that because something is performed it does not convey "real" information is to force oneself into a needlessly confining box ... as ethnomethodology and ethnography of communication research made abundantly clear many years ago, culturally specified, learned, rehearsed, performative routines (in physical and verbal actions) are part of what make life both predictable and intelligible.... . Performances *are* culturally telling and revealing.
>
> (p. 255)

But there are other potential problems as well. As MacDougal (1991) has noted, in many cultures a person's name and image should not be uttered or shown after his or her death. In other cases there is secret sacred knowledge that is not to be shared with the uninitiated or with one gender or the other. This can often be respected by taking down or restricting or forbidding access in museum displays, but it is a more troublesome issue with open Internet access to digitized representations (Belk and Groves 1999). Even if a representation is taken down from the Internet, this is no guarantee that it has not been copied and redistributed by someone else.

Additional types of visual collaborations

Most of the preceding discussion has focused on visual collaborations with informants. But there are other stakeholders with whom researchers may collaborate. Chief among them are the audiences or clients who consume the research output. In both academic and corporate research, attention has increasingly turned to business, consumers, and the digital world that is so much a part of contemporary consumption (e.g., Coleman 2009, 2010; Fortun 2012; Horst and Miller 2006; Humphrey 2009; Malefyt 2009; Miller and Horst 2012; Miller and Slater 2000; Mills and Ratcliffe 2012; Pink 2004; Suchman 2007). These shifts have resulted from following the growing part of our lives spent with digital consumption as well from pressures within academia (Mills and Radcliffe 2012) and employment and funding opportunities for both academic and commercial ethnographers (Malefyt 2009; Pink 2004). Further visual ethnographic collaborations have been found with the field of design (Attfield 2000; Crabtree 2003; Crabtree and Rodden 2002; Crabtree, Rouncefield, and Tolmie 2012; Gunn and Donovan 2012). One result for commercial ethnographers has been a shift in methods toward the visual and "fast ethnography" as well as a shift in the unit of analysis from society and culture to the individual (Malefyt 2009). Whether this demand-driven change weakens the value of resulting ethnographies and leads to an over-reliance on the visual is an important topic, but one which is too complex to be considered here.

Greater attention to audiences has also resulted in new, more collaborative forms of sharing information. As Oliveira (2013) emphasizes, it is important to engage corporate clients in the field by inviting their presence at field sites as well as enlisting them to help interpret edited presentations of visual and other ethnographic data. This creates client "buy-in" to findings as well as active participation in deriving implications. It is also useful to create interactive media presentations of results on DVD or the Internet (Belk 1998; Kershenboom 1995) as well as in "graphic facilitation" in which PowerPoint presentations are replaced by interactive live drawing of visual representations (McGinn 2010). Drawing on Fiske (1994), Rose (2001) calls this *audiencing*, meaning "the process by which a visual image has its meanings renegotiated, or even rejected, by particular audiences watching in specific circumstances" (p. 55).

Even when the indigenous audience is in another part of the world, such sharing can also virtually repatriate collected objects. An example is the British Museum's online interactive presentation of an Australian bark shield obtained by Captain Cook in 1770. A remote audience of Aboriginal Australians performed an interpretive dance and discussion in response once the shield was "released from its glass case" where it was physically stored (Hogsden and Poulter 2012). A number of other examples of virtually repatriating collected objects can be found in Christen (2011).

Conclusions

This has necessarily been an incomplete look at the imperatives for and challenges with using collaborative visual research in a consumption context. Additional issues include how to stimulate polyvocal dialogic representations (for a good discussion in the context of Dennis O'Rourke's *Cannibal Tours*, see MacCannell 1990). There are also questions of who is in front of and who is behind the camera, as in some of Jean Rouch's films (see Ruby 2000 for a discussion). We should also consider the fact that empowering the subjects of a project to engage in self-representation creates another truth, but not necessarily a "truer" truth. We found in showing our account of a flea-market ethnography (Belk, Sherry, and Wallendorf 1988) to a subset of participants, that they insisted that the stolen merchandise that we found present was extremely rare. Our experience suggested otherwise, but we wound up leaving such evidence out of our published account. Men's perspectives may also dominate women's or dominant social classes may shut out subordinate social class representations in a number of cultures (Banks 2001). That is, self-depictions can also be problematic. Nevertheless, as Pink (2001) points out, we still learn something about how people wish to represent themselves.

Even with good collaborative research intentions, some of the same power imbalances that operate in non-collaborative research may still be present.

For example, powerful groups are more likely to deny access to researchers or to be willing to represent themselves, for they are often already well represented and may wish to keep a low profile from outsiders whom they know may have a critical perspective (Low 2004; Marcus 1983; Prosser and Schwartz 1998). This does not mean that it is impossible to study "upward," but it can be more difficult than studying "downward." Gaining access is still possible, but it often takes additional work and cleverness (e.g., see Goldberg 1985). Janeen Costa and I (Costa and Belk 1990) found that we had to continuously adjust appointments in order to study an extended nouveau riche family and that while our video equipment might impress poorer consumers, it was critiqued as not being the very latest thing by members of this family. There are many technical issues in visual studies including what to film, how to frame shots, how to film, how to edit, and many other key decisions that affect what the audience sees in the images we create, co-create, and present (e.g, see Barbash and Taylor 1997; Marion and Crowder 2013). However, space does not allow a discussion of these key decisions here.

Representation can never be and should never be an objective and value-free project (Hamilton 1997). Even with the flood of available images from CCTV cameras around the world, we must still choose images and decide what we will do with them. There are also further ethical issues to consider as new technologies make possible new data collection techniques. For example, it is legal, but clearly unethical, for retailers to use their in-store surveillance video recorders to identify shoppers using facial recognition software, to instantly tie people into their purchase and credit histories, and to feed this information to store clerks who can try to upsell customers the merchandise these records suggest they may find most appealing (Belk, Fischer, and Kozinets 2013). Stores can also trace shopper in-store shopping patterns using traces from their mobile phones, even when they are not on. This can provide unobtrusive evidence of how long they spend in various aisles and parts of the store, but it also raises new ethical questions. Some of the same advanced technologies that potentially empower marginalized groups can also be used to disempower and exploit them. These are among the deeper issues that we need to consider in a digital age.

References

Agee, J., & Evans, W. (1941). *Let Us Now Praise Famous Men*. Boston: Houghton Mifflin.

Allen, E. (2013). *Update on the Twitter archive at the Library of Congress*. Library of Congress Blog, http://blogs.loc.gov/loc/2013/01/update-on-the-twitter-archive-at-the-library-of-congress

Alvelos, H. (2004). The Desert of Imagination in the City of Signs: Cultural Implications of Sponsored Transgression and Branded Graffiti. In J. Ferrell, K. Hayward, W. Morrison, & M. Presdee (Eds.), *Cultural Criminology Unleashed*, London: Glasshouse Press, 181–191.

Attfield, J. (2000). *Wild Things: Material Culture in Everyday Life*. Oxford: Berg.

Banks, M. (2001). *Visual Methods in Social Research*. London: SAGE.

Banksy. (2006). *Wall and Piece*. London: Century.

Banksy. (2010), *Exit Through the Gift Shop*. 87 minutes, London: Revolver Entertainment.

Barbash, I., & Taylor, L. (1997). *Cross-Cultural Filmmaking: A Handbook for Making Documentary and Ethnographic Films and Videos*, Berkeley, CA: University of California Press.

Barthes, R. (1977). Rhetoric of the Image. In R. Barthes, *Image-Music-Text*. S. Heath, trans. New York: Hill & Wang, 33–51.

Belk, R. (1998). Multimedia Approaches to Qualitative Data and Representations. In B. Stern (Ed.), *Representing Consumers: Voices, Views, and Visions*, London: Routledge, 308–338.

Belk, R. (2000). Consumption Patterns of the New Elite in Zimbabwe. In C. J. Shultz II & B. Grbac (Eds.), *Marketing Contributions to Democratization and Socioeconomic Development*, Rijeka, Croatia: Sveu Knjiznica, 120–137.

Belk, R. (2010). Representing the Global Consumer: Desire, Possessions, and Identity. In P. Maclaran, M. Saren, B. Stern, & M. Tadajewski, (Eds.), *The SAGE Handbook of Marketing Theory*, Thousand Oaks, CA: SAGE, 283–298.

Belk, R. (2013). Extended Self in a Digital World. *Journal of Consumer Research*, October, 40.

Belk, R. (2014). Sharing versus Pseudo-Sharing in Web 2.0. *The Anthropologist*, 4(2).

Belk, R., & Groves, R. (1999). Marketing and the Multiple Meanings of Aboriginal Art. *Journal of Macromarketing*. 19, June, 20–33.

Belk, R. W., & Kozinets, R. V. (2005). Videography in Marketing and Consumer Research. *Qualitative Market Research*, 8(2), 141–153.

Belk, R., & Yeh, J. (2011). Tourist Photography: Signs of Self. *International Journal of Culture, Tourism, and Hospitality*, 5(1), 345–353.

Belk, R., Fischer, E., & Kozinets, R. (2013). *Qualitative Consumer & Marketing Research*. London: SAGE.

Belk, R., Ger, G., & Askegaard, S. (2003). The Fire of Desire: A Multi-sited Inquiry into Consumer Passion. *Journal of Consumer Research*, 30, December, 326–351.

Belk, R., Sherry, J., Jr., & Wallendorf, M. (1988). A Naturalistic Inquiry into Buyer and Seller Behavior at a Swap Meet. *Journal of Consumer Research*, 14(4), 449–470.

Best, S., & Krueger, B. (2002). *Internet Data Collection*. Thousand Oaks, CA: SAGE.

Boellstorff, T. (2008). *Coming of Age in Second Life: An Anthropologist Explores the Virtually Human*. Princeton, NJ: Princeton University Press.

Braester, Y. (2011). Excuse Me, Your Camera is in my Face: Auturial Intervention in PRC New Documentary. In C. Berry, X. Lu, & L. Rofel (Eds.), *The New Chinese Documentary Film Movement: For the Public Record*, Hong Kong: Hong Kong University Press, 195–216.

Bruner, J. (2002). *Making Stories: Law Literature, Life*. Cambridge, MA: Harvard University Press.

Burgess, J., & Green, J. (2009). *YouTube: Online Video and Participatory Culture*. Cambridge: Polity Press.

Burnett, R. (2004). *How Images Think*. Cambridge, MA: MIT Press.

Cayla, J., & Arnould, E. (2013). Ethnographic Stories for Market Learning. *Journal of Marketing*, 77, July, 1–16.

Cayla, J., Beers, R., & Arnould, E. (2014). Stories the Deliver Business Insights. *MIT Sloan Management Review*, 55(2), 55–62.

Chalfen, R. (1987). *Snapshot Versions of Life*. Bowling Green, OH: Bowling Green State University Popular Press.

Chalfen, R. (1988). Home Video Versions of Life – Anything New? *Society for Visual Anthropology Newsletter*, 4(2), 1–5.

Chalfen, R. (1998). Interpreting Family Photography as Pictorial Communication. In J. Prosser, (Ed.), *Image-based Research: A Sourcebook for Qualitative Researchers*, London: Routledge Falmer, 214–234.

Christen, K. (2011). Opening Archives: Respectful Repatriation. *American Archivist*, 74, Spring-Summer, 185–210.

Clifford, J. (1988). *The Predicament of Culture: Twentieth-Century Ethnography, Literature, and Art*. Cambridge, MA: Harvard University Press.

Clifford, J., & Marcus, G. (Eds.) (1986). *Writing Culture: The Poetics and Politics of Ethnography*. Berkeley, CA: University of California Press.

Coleman, G. (2009). The Hacker Conference: A Ritual Condensation and Celebration of a Lifeworld. *Anthropological Quarterly*, 77, 507–519.

Coleman, G. (2010). Ethnographic Approaches to Digital Media. *Annual Review of Anthropology*, 39, 487–505.

Corneiliussen, H., & Rettberg, J. (Eds.) (2011). *Digital Culture, Play, and Identity: A World of Warcraft Reader*. Cambridge, MA: MIT Press.

Costa, J., & Belk, R. (1990). Nouveaux Riches as Quintessential Americans: Case Studies in an Extended Family. In R. Belk (Ed.), *Research in Consumer Behavior*, Greenwich, CT: JAI Press, 83–140.

Crabtree, A. (2003). *Designing Collaborative Systems: A Practical Guide to Ethnography*. New York: Springer.

Crabtree, A., & Rodden, T. (2002). Ethnography and Design? *Proceedings of the International Workshop on Interpretive Approaches to Information Systems and Computing Research*, Association of Information Systems, 70–74.

Crabtree, A., Rouncefield, M., & Tolmie, P. (2012). *Doing Design Ethnography*. New York: Springer.

David, B., & Wilson, M. (2002). Spaces of Resistance: Graffiti and Indigenous Place Markings in the Early European Contact Period in Northern Australia. In B. David & M. Wilson (Eds.), *Inscribed Land: Marking and Making Place*, Honolulu, HI: University of Hawaii Press, 42–60.

Dean, J. (2010). *Blog Theory*. Cambridge: Polity.

Drenton, J. (2012). Snapshots of the Self: Exploring the Role of Online Mobile Photo Sharing in Identity Development among adolescent girls. In A. Close (Ed.), *Online Consumer Behavior: Theory and Research in Social Media, Advertising, and E-Tail*, New York: Routledge, 3–34.

Drew, S., & Guillemin, M. (2014). From Photographs to Findings: Visual Meaning-Making and Interpretive Engagement in the Analysis of Participant-Generated Images. *Visual Studies*, 29(1), 54–67.

Elliott, J. (2005). *Using Narrative in Social Research: Qualitative and Quantitative Approaches*. London: SAGE.

Emmanuel, D. (2007). Making Public Space through a Renewed Cultural Activism. In G. Stanczak (Ed.), *Visual Research Methods: Image, Society, and Representation*, Los Angeles, CA: SAGE, 225–254.

Emmison, M., & Smith, P. (Eds.) (2000). *Researching the Visual: Images, Objects, Contexts and Interactions in Social and Cultural Inquiry*. London: SAGE.

Ferrell, J. (1995). Urban Graffiti: Crime, Control and Resistance. *Youth and Society*, 27(1), 73–92.

Fiske, J. (1994). Audiencing: Cultural Practice and Cultural Studies. In N. Denzin and Y. Lincoln, (Eds.), *Handbook of Qualitative Methods*. London: SAGE, 189–198.

Flaherty, R. (1922). *Nanook of the North*. 79-minutes, St. Johns, NFL: Les Frères Revillon.

Fortun, K. (2012). Ethnography in Late Industrialism. *Cultural Anthropology*, 27(3), 446–464.

Furlong, R. (1995). There's No Place Like Home. In M. Lister (Ed.), *The Photographic Image in Digital Culture*, London: Routledge, 170–187.

Gardner, R., & Östör, Á. (2001). *Making Forest of Bliss: Intention, Circumstance, and Chance in Nonfiction Film*. Cambridge, MA: Harvard University Press.

Goldberg, J. (1985). *Rich and Poor*. New York: Random House.

Guillemin, M., & S. Drew (2010). Questions of Process in Participant-Generated Visual Methodologies. *Visual Studies*, 25(2), 175–188.

Gunn, W., & Donovan, J. (2012). *Design and Anthropology*, Farnham, UK: Ashgate.

Hagen, C. (1985). *American Photographers of the Depression*. New York: Pantheon.

Hamilton, P. (1997). Representing the Social: France and Frenchness in Post-war Humanist Photography. In S. Hall (Ed.), *Representation: Cultural Representations and Signifying Practices*. London: SAGE, 75–150.

Heider, K. (1997). *Seeing Anthropology: Cultural Anthropology through Film*. Boston: Allyn & Bacon.

Heisley, D., & Levy, S. (1991). Autodriving: A Photoelicitation Technique. *Journal of Consumer Research*. 18(3), 257–272.

Hirsch, J. (1981). *Family Photographs: Content, Meaning and Effect*. New York: Oxford University Press.

Hocking, B. (2012). Beautiful Barriers: Art and Identity along a Belfast 'Peace' Wall. *Anthropology Matters*, 14(1). www.anthropologymatters.com/index.php?journal =anth_matters&page=article&op=viewArticle&path%5B%5D =273&path%5B%5D=451

Hogsden, C., & Poulter, E. (2012). The Real Other? Museum Objects in Digital Contact Networks. *Journal of Material Culture*. 17 (3), 265–286.

Holliday, R. (2007). Performance, Confessions and Identities: Using Video Diaries to Research Sexualities. In G. Stanczak (Ed.), *Visual Research Methods: Image, Society, and Representation*. Los Angeles, CA: SAGE, 255–279.

Holmes, D., & Marcus, G. (2006). Fast Capitalism: Para-ethnography and the Rise of the Symbolic Analyst. In M. Fisher and G. Downey (Eds.), *Frontiers of Capital: Ethnographic Reflections on the New Economy*. Durham, NC: Duke University Press, 33–57.

Holmes, D., & Marcus, G. (2008). Collaboration Today and the Re-imagination of the Classic Scene of Fieldwork Encounter. *Collaborative Anthropologies*, 1, 81–101.

Horst, H., & D. Miller. (2006). *The Cell Phone: An Anthropology of Communication.* Oxford: Berg.

Humphrey, C. (2009). The Mask and the Face: Imagination and Social Life in Russian Chat Rooms and Beyond. *Ethnos, 74,* 31–50.

Hussin, M., Frazier, S., & Thompson, J. (2011). Fat Stigmatization on YouTube: A Content Analysis. *Body Image, 8*(1), 90–92.

Izhizuka, K., & Zimmermann, P. (Eds.). (2008). *Mining the Home Movie: Excavations in Histories and Memories.* Berkeley, CA: University of California Press.

Jackson, B., & Ives, E. (Eds.) (1996). *The World Observed: Reflections on the Fieldwork Process.* Urbana, IL: University of Illinois Press.

Jensen, L. (2004). The Photographs of Jacob Riis: History in Relation to Truth. *Constructing the Past, 5*(1). http://digitalcommons.iwu.edu/constructing/vol5/iss1/6

John, N. A. (2012). Sharing and Web 2.0: The Emergence of a Keyword. *New Media and Society.* http://nms.sagepub.com/content/early/2012/07/03/1461444812450684doi:10.1177/1451444812450684

Johns, M., Chen, S. -L., & Hall, G. (Eds.) (2004). *Online Social Research: Methods, Issues, & Ethics.* New York: Peter Lang.

Keats, P. (2009). Multiple Text Analysis in Narrative Research: Visual, Written, and Spoken Stories of Experience. *Qualitative Research, 9*(2), 181–195.

Kershenboom, S. (1995). *Word, Sound, Image: The Life of the Tamil Text,* Oxford: Berg.

King, G. (1984). *Say "Cheese"! Looking at Snapshots in a New Way.* New York: Dodd, Mead.

Kozinets, R. V. (2010). *Netnography: Doing Ethnographic Research Online.* London: SAGE.

Kozinets, R. V., & Belk, R. W. (2006). Camcorder society: Videography in Consumer and Marketing Research. In R. Belk (Ed.), *Handbook of Qualitative Research Methods in Marketing.* Cheltenham, UK: Edward Elgar, 335–344.

Lange, D. (1981). *Dorothea Lange.* New York: Aperture Foundation.

Lapenta, F. (2011). Goemedia: On Location-based Media: The Changing Status of Collective Image Production and the Emergence of Social Navigation Systems. *Visual Studies, 26*(1), 14–24.

Lassiter, L. (2005). Collaborative Ethnography and Public Anthropology. *Current Anthropology, 46*(1), 83–106.

Lesy, M. (1973). *Wisconsin Death Trip.* New York: Random House.

Lister, M. (1995). *The Photographic Image in Digital Culture.* London: Routledge.

Low, S. (2004). *Behind the Gates: Life, Security, and the Pursuit of Happiness in Fortress America.* London: Routledge.

Lutz, C., & Collins, J. (1993). *Reading National Geographic.* Chicago: University of Chicago Press.

MacCannell, D. (1990). Cannibal Tours. *Visual Anthropology Review, 6*(2), 14–24.

MacDougal, D. (1991). Whose Story Is It? *Visual Anthropology Review, 7*(2), 2–10.

McGinn, D. (2010). Tired of PowerPoint? Try this Instead. *Harvard Business Review, 88*(9), 30–31.

Malefyt, T. (2009). Understanding the Rise of Consumer Ethnography: Branding Technomethodologies in the New Economy. *American Anthropologist, 111*(2), 201–210.

Marion, J., & Crowder J. (2013). *Visual Research: A Concise Introduction to Thinking Visually.* London: Bloomsbury.

Marcus, G. (Ed.). (1983). *Elites: Ethnographic Issues.* Albuquerque, NM: University of New Mexico Press.

Marcus, G. (2012). Opinion: What Business Anthropology Is, What It Might Become … and What, Perhaps It Should Not Be. *Journal of Business Anthropology, 1*(2), 265–272.

Marcus, G., & Fisher, M. (Eds.) (1986). *Anthropology as Cultural Critique: An Experimental Movement in the Human Sciences.* Chicago: University of Chicago Press.

Martin, J. (2008). Consumer Code: Use-Value, Exchange-Value, and the Role of Virtual Goods in Second Life. *Journal of Virtual Worlds Research, 1*(2), 2–21.

Mendelson, A., & Papacharissi, Z. (2011). Look at Us: Collective Narcissism in College Student Facebook Photo Galleries. In Z. Papacharissi, (Ed.), *A Networked Self: Identity, Community, and Culture on Social Network Sites,* New York: Routledge, 253–273.

Miller, D. (2011). *Tales from Facebook.* Cambridge: Polity Press.

Miller, D., & Horst, H. (2012). The Digital and the Human: A Prospectus for Digital Anthropology. In D. Miller & H. Horst (Eds.), *Digital Anthropology,* Oxford: Berg, 3–35.

Miller, D., & Slater, D. (2000). *The Internet: An Ethnographic Approach.* Oxford: Berg.

Mills, D., & Ratcliffe, R. (2012). After Method? Ethnography in the Knowledge Economy. *Qualitative Research, 12*(2), 147–164.

Murthy, D. (2008). Doing Ethnography: An Examination of the Use of New Technologies for Social Research. *Sociology, 42*(5), 837–855.

Nguyen, D., & Belk, R. (2007). This We Remember: Consuming Representation in Remembering. *Consumption, Markets and Culture, 10*(3), 251–291.

Odom, W., Zimmerman, J., & Forlizzi, J. (2011). Teenagers and their Virtual Possessions: Design

Oliveira, P. (2013). *People-Centered Innovation: Becoming a Practitioner in Innovation Research.* Columbus, OH: Biblio.

Opportunities and Issues. *CHI 2011,* May 7–12, Vancouver, BC, Canada, 1491–1500.

Pace, S. (2012). Citizens in YouTube: Research Methods Issues. In C. Silva (Ed.), *Online Research Methods in Urban and Planning Studies: Design and Outcomes.* Hershey, PA: Information Science Reference, 249–261.

Page, J. (2005). *Towards a Theory of Visual Narrative Analysis: What We See on HGTV.* Columbia, MO: University of Missouri Press.

Pearce, C., & Artemesia. (2009). *Communities of Play: Emergent Cultures in Multiplayer Games and Virtual Worlds.* Cambridge, MA: MIT Press.

Pimenta, S., & Poovaiah, R. (2010). On Defining Visual Narratives. *Design Thoughts,* August, 25–46.

Pink, S. (2001). *Doing Visual Ethnography,* London: SAGE.

Pink, S. (2004). Introduction: Situating Visual Research. In S. Pink, K. László, & A. Afonso (Eds.), *Working Images: Visual Research and Representation in Ethnography.* London: Routledge, 1–12.

Pink, S. (2007). Walking with Video. *Visual Studies,* December, 240–252.

Pink, S. (2011a). Amateur Photographic Practice, Collective Representation and the Constitution of Place. *Visual Studies*, 6(2), 92–101.

Pink, S. (2011b). Sensory Digital Photography: Re-thinking 'Moving' and the Image. *Visual Studies*, March, 4–13.

Pink, S., Hubbard, P., O'Neill, M., & Radley, A. (2010). Walking Across Disciplines: From Ethnography to Arts Practice. *Visual Studies*, 25(1), 1–7.

Pinney, C. (1997). *Camera Indica: The Social Life of Indian Photographs*. Chicago: University of Chicago Press.

Prosser, J., & Schwartz, D. (1998). Photographs within the Sociological Research Process. In J. Prosser (Ed.), *Image-based Research: A Sourcebook for Qualitative Researchers*, London: Routledge, 115–130.

Rabiger, M. (2009). *Directing the Documentary* (5th ed.). Stoneham, MA: Focal Press.

Renov, M. (1996). Video Confessions. In M. Renov and E. Suderburg (Eds.), *Resolutions: Contemporary Video Practices*. Minneapolis, MN: University of Minnesota Press, 78–101.

Rettberg, J. (1988). *Blogging*. Cambridge: Polity.

Riessman, C. (1993). *Narrative Analysis*. Newbury Park, CA: SAGE.

Riessman, C. (2008). *Narrative Methods for the Human Sciences*. Thousand Oaks, CA: SAGE.

Riis, J. (1890/1986). *How the Other Half Lives*. Boston: Bedford Books.

Rook, D. (1985). *Consumers' Video Archives and Household Rituals*. Paper presented at Association for Consumer Research Annual Conference, Las Vegas, NV.

Rose, G. (2001). *Visual Methodologies*. London: SAGE.

Ruby, J. (2000). *Picturing Culture: Explorations of Film & Anthropology*. Chicago: University of Chicago Press.

Schirato, T., & Webb, J. (2004). *Understanding the Visual*. London: SAGE.

Schroeder, J. E. (2002). *Visual Consumption*. London: Routledge.

Serfaty, V. (2004). *The Mirror and the Veil: An Overview of American Online Diaries and Blogs*. Amsterdam: Rodopi.

Shove, E., Watson, M., Hand, M., & Ingram, J. (2007). *The Design of Everyday Life*. Oxford: Berg.

Sobh, R., & Belk, R. (2011a). Domains of Privacy and Hospitality in Arab Gulf Homes. *Journal of Islamic Marketing*, 2(2), 125–137.

Sobh, R., & Belk, R. (2011b). Gender Privacy in Arab Gulf States: Implications for Consumption and Marketing. In Ö. Sandicki and G. Rice (Eds.), *Handbook of Islamic Marketing*. Cheltenham, UK: Edward Elgar, 73–96.

Sobh, R., & Belk, R. (2011c). Privacy and Gendered Spaces in Arab Gulf Homes. *Home Cultures*, 8(3), 317–340.

Sobh, R., & Belk, R. (forthcoming). Modest Seductiveness: Reconciling Modesty and Vanity by Reverse Assimilation and Double Resistance. *Journal of Consumer Behavior*.

Stephens, M. (1998). *The Rise of the Image and the Fall of the Word*. Oxford: Oxford University Press.

Strangelove, M. (2010). *Watching YouTube: Extraordinary Videos by Ordinary People*. Toronto: University of Toronto Press.

Suchman, L. (2007). *Anthropology as 'Brand': Reflections on Corporate Anthropology*. Paper presented at the Colloquium on Interdisciplinarity and

Society, Oxford University, 24 February. www.lancaster.ac.uk/sociology/research/publications/papers/suchman-anthropology-asbrand.pdf

Suler, J. (2004). The Online Disinhibition Effect. *The Psychology of Cyberspace*, August, (v3.0). http://users.rider.edu/~suler/psycyber/disinhibit.html

Sunderland, P. L., & Denny, R. M. (2007). *Doing Anthropology in Consumer Research*. Walnut Creek, CA: Left Coast Press.

Tian, K., & Belk, R. (2005). Extended Self and Possessions in the Workplace. *Journal of Consumer Research*, 32(2), 297–310.

Van Maanen, J. (1988), *Tales of the Field: On Writing Ethnography*. Chicago: University of Chicago Press.

Vicente, P., Reis, E., & Santos, M. (2009). Using Mobile Phones for Survey Research: A Comparative Analysis between Data Collected via Mobile Phones and Fixed Phones. *International Journal of Market Research*, 51(5), 1–21.

Visconti, L., Sherry, J., Borghini, S., & Anderson, L. (2010). Street Art, Sweet Art? Reclaiming the "Public" in Public Place. *Journal of Consumer Research*, 37(3), 511–529.

Walker, I. (1995). Desert Stories or Faith in Facts? In M. Lister (Ed.), *The Photographic Image in Digital Culture*. London: Routledge, 236–252.

Wesch, M. (2008). An Anthropological Introduction to YouTube. June 23, www.youtube.com/watch?v=TPAO-lZ4_hU

Wesolowski, A., & N. Eagle. (2012). Mobile Phones as a Lens into Slum Dynamics. In C. Silva (Ed.), *Online Research Methods in Urban and Planning Studies: Design and Outcomes*. Hershey, PA: Information Science Reference, 334–352.

7 Backyard ethnography

Defamiliarizing the familiar and understanding the consumer

Inga Treitler

"An object is not so attached to its name that one cannot find for it another which is more suitable."

(René Magritte, 1929)

Introduction

The truly unfamiliar does not exist – not for long anyway. Magritte delighted in challenging the public through his art to defamiliarize familiar things. An everyday object, a pipe, say, is not what we think it is [*ceci n'est pas une pipe*]. To challenge our assumptions, he suggests, is to bring new depths of thought, if not knowledge (Cembalest, 2012). Mental model theory, which informs much of the analysis in this chapter, teaches us that both too much familiarity and too little familiarity can be blinding. This is a chapter about several ways that observers can work with the familiar without succumbing to the comfortable assumptions that can obscure what is in front of us to be seen and experienced. "Untamed subjectivity," writes a sociologist of education "mutes the emic voice" (Peshkin, 1988: 21). As his work suggests, the literature on how we shape our research through the facts of our life experiences, is broad, not restricted to anthropology, and serves a range of topics and applications, from theory to increasing arenas of practice. In the arenas of practice is where this chapter is situated in hopes of stimulating a conversation about how to bring consumers more into the research and how to continue to engage clients as collaborators in research. The last twenty years have seen many breakthrough technologies and methods, from the simple pencil and paper to the sophisticated applications of information technology for bringing consumers and clients into research. Many of these state-of-the-art developments can be found in the proceedings of the Ethnographic Praxis in Industry Conference (see, for example, EPIC2013's session, (Co)creation and (Co)participation: multiple actors in research epiconference.com, introduced by Ortlieb 2013).

Backyard ethnography is not, to say the least, a neglected topic, as has been noted in van Maanen (2011) in what he calls the proliferation of adjectival anthropology. There's an established and rich literature on native anthropology, insider anthropology, feminist anthropology, reflexivity, positionality, and studying up, all of which involve working in familiar environments and questioning the researcher position in shaping understandings. Issues addressed concern cultural identity, power, race, oppression, and privilege. Though these questions will never be irrelevant in any ethnographic encounter the driving concern for this essay is to anchor an understanding of how to pre-emptively minimize bias that may interfere with perception of critical differences among mental or cultural models. (I use the terms *mental model* and *cultural model* interchangeably; I avoid *cognitive model*, though the theoretical foundations are from cognitive and psychological anthropologists.)

The theoretical foundations that shape this chapter have roots in cognitive anthropology and mental model theory, and that comes with a particular focus on the science of perception and communication, and these are addressed in a section on deconstructing participant observation. The remainder of the chapter is structured as follows. First, three kinds of backyard ethnography are presented, with examples from each. The largest portion of the discussion is on the very immersive and personal experience of my community interviews. I give greater attention to those vignettes because the researcher point of view is mine, so I have access to the subjectivity and biases, whereas the cases for consumer as ethnographer and the client as ethnographer are about the mechanics of creating space for these collaborations with a cautionary note about the risks for bias. In those cases we had only limited ways to train the collaborators to be alert to their own biases. That topic is taken up again in the final section of the chapter. Second, I recapture and deconstruct the elements of traditional participant observation, because that is the point at which our ideologies and our own mental models stand to influence not just our field interactions but what we notice and what gets recorded. The final section is about how parties within organizations can use the defamiliarization tips to explore their own assumptions about their products, to integrate the consumer interests into thinking about their products, and as is a pattern on the rise in organizational transformation, to include diverse internal perspectives on the products and on the organization itself.

Three kinds of backyard ethnography

First, we anthropologists can, and increasingly do, counter to orthodoxy, study close to home. In fact it's not terribly new, in the sense that even the traditional Malinowskian method of participant observation rested on the pillars of "rapport" and "entrée" key components of recreating a "homelike" context. In the "Community Ethnography" section, three vignettes from the mental-models interviews about learning are presented. Second, the respondent can be the ethnographer – the ultimate insider, using their eyes and ears and senses and perceptions to frame and collect the story and share it with the anthropologist. In this section, I describe a pioneering undertaking for the U.S. Department of Energy that involved paying recipients in an entitlement program to interview their friends and family to collect remembered stories about the program. And finally, researchers can take the client into the backyard with them. For this section, I describe collaboration with a fast food client who shadowed the ethnographer.

1. Community ethnography

As van Maanen intones in his 2011 edition of *Tales of the Field*, "Backyard ethnography has not often had the approval of priests" though, he goes on to note, "change is afoot" (p. 41). And so it is. About a year ago, I was invited to interview some "ordinary Americans" to hear their opinions on what they think is important to learn, and how they think learning best takes place. Selection criteria excluded educators or those involved in education policy, but were otherwise a broad cross section of ages, gender, and occupations. The client is the Frameworks Institute; a Washington DC-based nonprofit group that does applied communications research for policy makers and members of the general public (frameworksinstitute.org). I mention their name with permission, but the interviews summarized in the vignettes are anonymized. The client's recruiter contacted me and together we looked at some local recruiting agencies, and I made some phone calls and then selected one that seemed well situated to meet our needs. The client provided the recruiting parameters and then the recruiter and I reviewed the list of respondents together to make sure they fit the goals of the interviews. All the other interviews around the country and in several non-U.S. countries are held in public places like malls, cafes, and restaurants. The interviews are long enough that it's nice for the participant to be able to get a drink or a bite to eat if it's mealtime. I selected a Starbucks in a central location, easy for people from outside the central city to find quickly, but a Starbucks where I don't go that often so there would be little risk of someone coming by whom I know. The goal of the interviews was to construct cultural models of tacit knowledge. The analysis will be presented to other nonprofits and policy makers to help them articulate messages that will be better understood by the public because they use familiar mental models. Interviews were conducted in several communities around the United States, each ethnographer doing interviews in their own communities.

Community ethnography's upsides

Backyard ethnography allows projects to economize on time, energy, and emotions. Researchers have greater control over recruitment and build on local community knowledge. Backyard ethnography allows researchers to share points of reference with the research participant (landmarks are familiar, local personalities are known). For example, in the conversations about education I was interested in non-classroom learning, and respondents made reference to places, events, and issues that I am familiar with: Ijams Nature Center (pronounced *iyams*), the World's Fair Park, Dollywood, trails in Smoky Mountain National Park, schools, fan-dom for the UT Vols, unequal access to the Internet in classrooms. Because the interviews were transcribed and the analysis was not done by me, I had to be sure that the participant explained what was important to them about each point of reference. That part of the interview turned into a helpful device. The particular combination here of interviews by a community member and analysis by a non-community member who also had no access to nonverbal cues, created something of an additional safeguard against insinuating bias.

Community ethnography's downsides

Asking for clarification and contextual and surrounding detail in an interview is absolutely standard, especially when looking for particular language, terms, turns of phrase, and the sorts of things that will reveal an underlying mental model – that point where things feel different and noteworthy, possessing a kind of theretofore unrecognized logic where our deeper questioning and circling around will be focused. But the prompts and probes are easier and more egalitarian when it comes from a place of really not knowing. So asking the question on behalf of the "unfamiliar" analyst who would only have transcribed interview notes (not even tape) to go by, that was useful. It also helped me not plough through assuming that because of shared references I understood the underlying meanings and values. Shared references can in fact be dangerous. They are not the same as shared experiences. It is easy to fall into a patter about Smoky Mountain trails, special events at Ijams. Stepping back and asking the respondent to speak to the remote analyst gave them a chance to really frame the reference according to what's important to them. It helps them articulate tacit knowledge and unconscious assumptions. The difficulty of objectivity is a recurrent theme in anthropology (e.g., Clifford and Marcus, 1986) and the risks of backyard ethnography are rooted in anthropology's canon. So here I am in a small community, facing down those risks.

Here's the context of the community ethnographies. Knoxville is a city of 200,000, with a county population of nearly 0.5 million that speaks to an urban-suburban split, and many small rural, isolated towns across the Tennessee Valley whose populations are dependent on Knoxville for commerce and medical facilities. By those figures it counts as a large city in the U.S., where average city size is 100,000. But its history and its valley geography have left it a segregated place where people live in small-town style within individual communities. I hasten to add that small-town living in big cities of the world is not unusual. Who says it better than the little boy of privilege from NYC's Upper East, one of the world's highest rent districts in *The Nanny Diaries*? "The Museum of Natural History?" he gasps,

"That's on the West side, isn't it? Mommy says never go on the West Side!" (McLaughlin and Kraus 2003). Small-town living anywhere poses challenges for backyard ethnography. For example, over the 25 years I've lived in Knoxville, the degrees of interpersonal separation have shrunk, even though local lore still names me a "damn Yankee" – that's the kind who comes from up north and never goes away. But even though "my people" aren't from here and I don't have a church, or maybe because of that, it does not take long to find common acquaintances. I list the degrees of separation as a downside, or maybe a potential obstacle is a better way to put it, because of the experience of Case #2 in the next section. Finding common acquaintances with the respondent in that interview gave me a feeling of camaraderie. Nice. But ethnographically risky. I felt we shared cultural models, but to presume we did would, as Peshkin (1988) put it, "mute the emic voice."

The ethnography consists of eight 90-minute interviews. The structure of the interview and the style of questions were prepared by the researchers at Frameworks, the client. The theoretical underpinnings of the survey design is from early cognitive anthropological and linguistic theory of cultural models (for example, Jackendoff, 1985; Holland and Quinn, 1987; Keller and Keller, 1996). The style of our conversations allows the participant's natural language, phrasing, timing, hesitations, tones of voice, and nonverbal enunciations like laughter to be part of the analysis, as captured in the transcription. The interviewer is not the person responsible for analyzing the transcripts and for reconstructing the cultural models. That is done by two other researchers, whose articulation of posited cultural models are discussed and then articulated as core cultural models. The idea is to find a way to identify from the general public, deeply held core beliefs expressed using their framing of personal experience and their recall of events in the news and in their communities. The use of multiple interpretations is intended to help minimize biases from each individual analyst, and also to eliminate the sort of deep personal connection that can develop in an interview when the ethnographer empathizes and that symbolic membrane between them becomes too porous to the point that the cultural models begin to merge. This multiple-analyst procedure separates the analysis from the individual respondent in a way that emphasizes underlying cultural knowledge. The progression of the conversation is ordered from broad to increasingly narrow, and the respondent is not told in advance what they will be discussing. In that way interviewers can be reasonably confident that the responses are spontaneous. During the interviews I took notes only to keep track of themes, not as a way to document. I kept the interview schedule in front of me but had key points highlighted so I only needed to glance down during our conversation to keep track of where we were in the progression. In the next section I describe a few characteristics of three different participants. Each one illustrates a different element of how I worked around the possible downsides of community ethnography and took advantage of the upsides.

Case #1

The middle-aged man walked toward me where I sat in the shade of an umbrella at the corner of the Starbucks next to the drive through station. The cars idling next to us had their windows rolled up and the heat from the engines moved the still air. It was a sultry summer day, but the music and the chatter of the other customers inside was going to make it hard to record so I staked out a table on the patio in the shade. His wife walked in just a step behind him, and after shaking my hand she went inside. She came back in a few minutes and without a word handed him a Frappuccino and slid into chair at the table next to us. At the time I wondered why she had stayed so nearby, but I was soon swept into conversation with her husband. Later she told me that it was her idea to sign him up to be interviewed for this study. She did it to help the recruiter, who, it happens, is a friend of hers. Small town. And, she also did it to help her husband. She thought it would be good for him, which I understand now. Taciturn is an understatement. He has no children of his own so to reflect on personal experience he went back some 40 years, and that took some thinking. He was raised in a remote county that has a long agricultural history. And that is where he still lives. He has the kind of leathery, slightly crinkly skin that comes with long hours in the sun. He worked from childhood helping his family farm. Everything he needed to learn for his career as a mechanic, he learned from working on his parents' tobacco farm – fixing the tractor, hanging out tobacco leaves, looking after livestock. "School was school, but the important stuff came from our farm." Except for his shop class and that is how he got a start as a mechanic. In a way he was the perfect "collaborator." He wanted to be part of the bigger conversation about education, even though he had no obvious vested interest in the outcome. The questions encouraged him to think about something he hadn't thought about in years, and put it into words. Not so easy, but as he told me later, very interesting to him. Talking didn't come easily for him. As he and his wife prepared to leave, in a perfect "doorknob" moment, that moment where, metaphorically speaking, her hand was on the doorknob as if preparing to leave, she instead sat down next to me in a familiar way that is rare here in Knoxville, where people are often more reserved until they "figure each other out." She asked me about my name, which is a combination of a Swedish first name and a German last name. She tells me she was born and raised in Germany and in 1970 she immigrated with her family at age 15 to Madison County where no one at school had ever met a German. She tells me that she did everything to strip away all remnants of a German accent. Though her mannerisms were a little different the accent was the distinct prosaic lilt of the East Tennessee mountains. She and her husband had only been married 5 years when I met them. Learning about her background was a neat bonus for me. It wouldn't be part of the transcription so it wouldn't contribute to building the mental models, because the tape was off. And it didn't change my understanding of his comments. But there had been something in the way the two of them came in together and the way she introduced herself to me and then sat nearby during the interview that made take notice and told me there was something unusual about them that led me to pace my questions differently and to not let the external cues of his gate, his dress, his deeply tanned, farmer's skin in early summer drop him in a box labeled Madison County Tobacco Farmer. His silences were expansive! Shy? Thoughtful? Confused?

Defamiliarizing Tips:

If something seems to be missing, approach the interview as a brand new never before seen cultural environment. Neglect visual cues that lead to stereotyping.

Take mental note of the institutional building blocks of the participant's life and visualize them – in this case, tractors, mechanics, the school building. Add flesh to the descriptions as if fiction writing until you can take them and anticipate what he might do there.

Case #2

With her bobbed gray hair, and her full gathered skirt, I knew from the moment she entered Panera that "she's not *from* these parts." She talked to me about the long road taken by the now largest public school in the region where her children had been students 10 years ago. Her husband had moved down from Washington DC, a lawyer with the Tennessee Valley Authority. Her neighborhood is known for its many Yankee "transplants" because the homes are older, the streets are tree-lined, and the property values are closer to those in the northeastern states. One of her sons has moved back north, and the other is struggling to find employment here in Knoxville. She has not taken paid work since arriving in Knoxville but spends lots of time volunteering with organizations that I'm familiar with and where I have acquaintances. My challenge here was to flip the switch that had already activated in my head – people we know in common, changes in the school system, community issues. It was hard to flip that switch back because in Knoxville more than in many other places, small symbols like hair color, clothing, and dialect are indicators that draw people together, or, alternatively, create a distance. The situation challenged me to not assume that I knew her or to empathize to the point of anticipating. It would be normal in daily life, and she and I might well have been friends. Instead I took that familiarity and turned it on its head, encouraging her to challenge her own assumptions and elaborate on her thoughts rather than think I understood. It is the common device used in ethnography of asking the research participant to assume the researcher really doesn't understand. We use any number of devices to get that dynamic. It doesn't always work, for example one respondent through up her hands in an interview and with exasperation in her voice said, "You really don't know much about this do you?!"

Defamiliarizing Tips:

Recognize nonverbal symbols that might draw ethnographer closer in a casual encounter. Those signals are starting points, not assumptions. Somehow avoid the bonding you might crave.

Hear the sequence of their presentation rather than probing based on shared assumptions. Here, I was not at my personal best. I had the visuals in my mind from the school, I even imagined her sons, wondering where they were and whether I knew them. As she mentioned an art center in downtown Knoxville, I thought of my friend who had built that center and trained many artists in the community. I confess that I shared her name with the respondent and if memory serves, I think we went onto a brief sidetrack full of accolades about this friend we shared history with. Did I miss a defamiliarizing opportunity? I believe I did. But the interview overall certainly did not suffer because we shared enough cues that she understood what the interview needed and went efficiently through her thoughts. What may have been missed are points of disagreement or counterintuitive notions that she may not have wanted to raise out of concern for the bond we had created. But I will not know.

Case #3

It was my fault. I had rejected one of the participants selected by the recruiters (that person was an educator, which disqualified her). I did not notice that the slot given to the replacement was a different time. So there I was, sitting at my computer downloading audio files from my little Sony recorder when the phone broke the silence of my empty office. It was the recruiter. The participant had just called him looking for me at the Starbucks where our meeting was scheduled. She'd been waiting 30 minutes. The thought in my mind was, what a patient woman, I would not have lasted that long! I quickly realized what had happened and scrambled to reach the cell phone that had my notes from the recruiter. She's a soccer mom, as it happens, and she tells me she "lives" in her SUV. The soccer fields where she was headed to meet her daughter after her practice are the same ones where I had spent countless (bored) hours of my life with my own children. Instinct told me to take off my work shoes and put on sneakers and a Puma athletic jacket, and to put on a swipe of lipstick. I jumped in the car and headed down the road past the familiar pastures and pulled in to the parking lot. I grabbed the recorder as she rolled down the window and waved. I smiled to see the red velour hoodie and matching warm up pants. Ha! Good instinct. She opened the passenger door to her Denali SUV, and I climbed up and perched on the passenger's seat. How great! I leaned back and sighed. We chattered away, just the way we soccer moms do. And I hadn't turned on the tape recorder yet. This is the "sigh and commiserate" part of the soccer mom thing. First we bond – number and ages of kids, kids' social and sports commitments, schools. I look at my watch and smile, and then I say, "Well shall we get started?" She touches her hair and I click on the recorder. Our sigh-and-commiserate discussion turns out to have worked extremely well because it gave me an instant frame of reference. She homeschools three children and a fourth one goes to a Christian private school. My homeschool fear. I silenced that mental tape and listened as she careened through one story after another of the "out of school" educational activities at Dollywood, at the zoo, at Ijams Nature Center, and all around the community joining with other Christian homeschooling parents. She told me that she's not comfortable with the public school so her children were withdrawn. "In science class they teach opinion as fact," she said, "and I don't think that's right." Why is it, I asked myself, that when I talk with people in other countries about religious beliefs different than mine, I listen and look for the system and the universality, and hooks begin to distinguish themselves, and cultural models take shape. But when I listen to someone in my town call evolution an opinion, I struggle turn off my internal tape. But I did, and that was the defamiliarization exercise. She continued her reflections on what it is like to learn the school material at the same time as her children are learning. I had asked her if she thought a different subject should be taught along with science and she had never considered that idea before so it helped her think deeply about her beliefs in how science should be taught. The question had thrown open an opportunity for her to put words to her beliefs. I thanked her for her time and for bringing many new perspectives to the conversation and clicked off the tape recorder. But she didn't want to stop talking. When I finally got into my sedan and pulled out of the parking lot I had not driven half a mile before my phone rang. She had just thought of some more ideas she wanted to tell me.

Defamiliarizing Tip:

This interview was emblematic of a cultural model just waiting to be articulated. The bonding was not a risk – we actually had nothing in common in our present life but I certainly understood her rhythms. The logic in her life was so clear to her because she had not had to step outside her frame much, as indicated by what happened when she did – when she perceived that her children were being badly educated because evolution was being taught in science. All she had to do was take over their education. It is interesting that when Frameworks told me about the interviews I had a momentary gasp. I called the client, and wondered if we should exclude homeschoolers. The decision was to not exclude them. And that was a perfect example of subjectivity thwarted! It turns out that homeschoolers have vast knowledge of the ways to take advantage of non-school resources for educating their children, and that is precisely the sort of thing we sought to extract during interviews. So when the participant takes the lead as in situations like this the mental models pour themselves and the more the ethnographer stays out of the way the more learning there is, remarkably, on both sides, as I realized when my phone rang on my drive home.

2. Consumer as ethnographer

In the opening paragraphs I said that clients and research participants will not replace anthropologists and ethnographers. The following demonstration study tested the use of consumers in recruiting information from within their own social networks. But ethnographers played a key role in selecting consumers and in training them for their role as consumer ethnographers studying their own environment.

A research team at Oak Ridge National Laboratory (ORNL) undertook an evaluation of one of the American Reconstruction and Recovery Act (ARRA) era programs for the U.S. Department of Energy (DOE). It was the National Weatherization Assistance Program, which provides financial assistance to those in need to improve the energy efficiency and health condition of their home. As part of the evaluation we sought to learn how information is shared within communities (potentially feeding a viral spread of interest). For this cohort we discovered very little social media activity so we invited the consumers to become researchers and collaborators. Each participant received an incentive payment. In a workshop we practiced open-ended interviewing. We helped the consumers think back on their experience with the program. Then we asked them to reflect on how they had communicated that to friends and family. What we asked them to do next was not easy. We asked them to defamiliarize their everyday relationships and to follow set communication topics, but to use their normal communication style. Ethnographers do this all the time. On the basis of these consumer ethnographer interviews we found that 46 percent of the people interviewed had taken action to contact their local program or make improvements on their own because of casual communication with friends and family (Rose and Hawkins, 2012). It is an important finding for a program that is intended to perpetuate household energy conservation behaviors. It was also a good test of using consumers to gather backyard data. As preliminary study this undertaking did not allow any follow-up with the consumer researchers who acted both as members of their community and observers of it. We are well aware that the "quality control" on the sorts of responses that are collected is very limited. Only at the front end, in the workshop, did we have an opportunity to be preemptive in helping the consumer internalize the behaviors associated with good listening, questioning, hearing, and note taking. But as a demonstration project it creates the possibility to extend the method into other arenas. For example, what might be the possibilities of truly creating new empathic and ethnographic ways of thinking and engaging among managers, as we will see in the "Client as Ethnographer" section?

The Weatherization Experience demonstration project was not, strictly speaking, business anthropology, so it was an interesting experience because I was able to create something of a bridge to extend methods from the public to the private sector applications of anthropology. Business anthropology has something of a longer history of using consumers to narrow the gap between researcher and consumer. Some ethnographers may remember the, at one time, highly innovative practice of using disposable cameras and journaling by consumers, even beeper studies, first made famous in the Experience Sampling studies of psychologist Csikszentmihalyi (1990). Collaging has a long history as a projective technique, used as a "homework" assignment or in focus-group settings for deeper understandings of specific products and brands. There is a proliferation of mobile apps and tools and a growing use of digital ethnography, social media, and phones with cameras and video. All are means for accessing a consumer's point of view and experience. These will only continue to increase as the general population has more access to smart phones, wearable technology, the Internet of Things, and applications of all of these that the consumer is often even more ingenious at developing than is the researcher.

3. Client as ethnographer

Clients in consumer ethnographies often ask to shadow ethnographic studies to get closer to the consumer. There are good reasons for them to be included and there are also good reasons for the ethnographer not to want them included. The latter is easily understood as cluttering the field. On the side of advantages to client inclusion there is nothing better for the product and for the company than for management to get firsthand experience (not just through a video or audio recording) of the lives of people who use the products. Typically the material the client is looking for is not like the applied communication research, which results in constructing a consumer's mental model. Rather the lived experience through story telling is the goal. Often the innovative mind of the user, as von Hippel *et al.* have shown (2011), identifies innovative uses among consumers of existing products – a pattern that is particularly common with computing technology. But there are constraints that this backyard ethnography discussion alerts us to. Clients, particularly in leadership, hold opinions of their product's "real" users and may feel a sort of ownership of the relationship. At that point the line from observation to socializing is crossed – that symbolic membrane separating consumer cultural models from researcher models is lost and the consumer model may be subsumed into the client's assumptions. The workaround many ethnographers will use in such cases to protect the data is to create a special window of opportunity for the client to follow on with questions not covered. And that is what we did in this case of a client shadowing for a fast food client.

The client's challenge was to find a way to increase the sales of their burgers among the group who were already real devotees of the brand. The study, conducted in several cities, consisted of in-home ethnographies and visits to several fast food restaurants (the client was anonymized). The method was new to the client, and many consumer ethnographer readers will recognize in this the client who is not just seeking to learn about the consumer but also seeking to learn some of the techniques of participant observation. The research team had worked with the client for over a year so it was agreed that each ethnographer would take one member of the client team to the field. As mentioned in the paragraph above in the section on "Consumer as Ethnographer," it's a good idea to have a plan. Here was where we began:

A brief tutorial was offered to explain how ethnography can be most successful:

- Be as non intrusive as possible – follow the respondent's lead on what is important to them;
- Make a social connection but do not allow your own personal narrative to get in the way; and
- Be friendly but don't "make friends" – that's the bonding issue that I encountered in the Community Ethnographies.

Field logistics:

- The team consists of two people: the ethnographer and the client.
- A request for an additional person from the client side was turned down because there's not enough space. The explanation was that because the study involved a drive to a fast food restaurant in the client's car, if the car was too small, the logistics would slow the project down.
- The study included videotaping – the client was given the responsibility of holding the video camera, and that way they were always a valued member of the team.
- The client was introduced as the cameraperson and a member of the team, not as the client.
- At predetermined moments, the ethnographer would check in with the client to see if they had topics that hadn't been addressed or if they were just curious about anything that had been brought up. If so, the client hands the camera to the ethnographer.

How did all this work? Not stellar in the field. There is an irresistible urge to bond. Sometimes the client was seen to step outside their "client" persona and a feeling of "who's cooler" would lurk. We speculated that might have something to do with the sense of authority the client feels, but it is also clearly the pride of ownership over the brand because of their dedication to the work over a long span of time, versus the relatively short engagement that the ethnography team typically has. However, in the project experience, when we ethnographers gathered in evenings with the client, the dinner conversation bubbled over with insights and experiences, anecdotes, surprises, and new understandings. Just the sort of thing ethnographic observations are intended to arrive at, so the added challenge of bringing a client to a deeper understanding of what it is to be and think ethnographically among consumers of the client's product is critical. The higher the level of management, moreover, the more avenues of communication that client has to convey understandings within the company about who the products and services are being developed for. And in the case of this study, there were more studies designed for our team in direct consequence of the growing appreciation for what is to be learned. Stories in the consumer and market anthropology community abound, though, of gaffes or awkward moments with clients in the field. Is it worth it? Each case must be assessed individually and the "boot camp" or tutorials designed as needed.

Deconstructing participant observation

I believe that one of the biggest challenges we are presented with when extending ethnography into the consumer- and the client-driven models has to do with the unexamined nature of observation itself (and of course participation as well, as indicated by the nearly irresistible urge to bond). What is it that we do when we are seeing things around us, and I refer the reader back to the unlinking of name and image by Magritte in the chapter's epigraph? As I delve into how we perceive, and by that I mean more than just see, but "take note," and mark as important, I also refer to the recognition of what we carry into our observation – the biases and subjectivities we've been talking about. The unexamined and tacit knowledge that is extracted by a skillful interview is also embedded in the interviewer and frames the sorts of things seen and noted.

The *backyard*, metaphorically, is anything that is in a researcher's comfort area. It could be we're engaged with clients and participants in the study of technology we have close working knowledge of, or that we share a life stage or role, like homeowner or parent. That used to be called *rapport*, so in a way this is not new at all. It's perhaps a new take on using our positioning, and carefully placing it in the ethnographic experience with enough self-awareness that we don't make assumptions about the degree of shared understandings. Being able to do that well, without directing, or monopolizing, is part of the super power that a good ethnographer possesses. The cases from the Community Interviews illustrate how theory of culture and cognition combine with "instinct" about meaningful patterns. Collaborative ethnography casts the consumer or the client as that backyard ethnographer, gathering knowledge from within their communities, or in the case of a client shadowing an ethnographer and observing sometimes for the first time, the consumer with the product.

In the introduction I mentioned that I worried about my biases on the topic of education, a very delicate topic here in East Tennessee, the buckle of the Bible belt. I wondered if my biases would show. I hold dearly to the idea that education is evidence and science based, and that religion is valuable but that it is practiced in spiritual communities, not in schools. I have long noticed that I have different ways of taking in new experiences in other countries where my mind is busy trying to build the mental models of those around me, versus in the U.S. where I consider myself at home and hold to "my ways." Elsewhere I am not bothered by invitations to people's churches like when I did research in the Caribbean; in the U.S. I feel proselytized to. Elsewhere I try new foods even if I think they're unhealthily loaded with sugar or unidentifiable ingredients like, like bubble tea in Singapore, for example. But I was also concerned about making assumptions about participants who were more aligned with me ideologically. Yet I was also excited to be in a place where I know the community, the landmarks, and the history and can bring experience and perspective to a more immediate understanding the participant's point of view. To be clear, I don't come from East Tennessee, so I bring something of an outsider's view even while being at home here for many years. This is a town that has not integrated new comers easily, as one could guess from the newly formed Knoxville New Yorkers Meetup group with members who have lived in Knoxville for decades. Will I carry an internal dialogue into my interviews? Will I assume things I shouldn't? Or perhaps be able to use it to my advantage for a more critical ear that hears better?

Observer

An internal dialogue can interfere with perception – feeling, seeing, smelling, hearing. An observer is never free of tacit knowledge, memories, assumptions, all of which influence perception. Observation is influenced by what we already know and how we define importance. Even the fact of observation is culturally determined. Not perceiving happens because it is so *familiar* we take it for granted or so *novel* we have no cultural model, or cognitive hooks to make sense of it. Either way one is blind.

Observation: Blinded by the familiar

Observation is the part of participant observation we rarely talk about, perhaps because it is taken for granted as a physiological process and we have sold short the cultural dimension. In fact it is a core cognitive and symbolic process. It consists of perceiving, representing, interpreting, analyzing, and then returning to test the initial perception. It is a dialectic. As cognitive scientist, Marvin Minsky, a pioneer of artificial intelligence, noted, "A theory of seeing should also be a theory of imagining" (Minsky, 1974). Perception also includes what is missed by the observer who decides it is *not* meaningful, or is distracted, or doesn't recognize a variant – or in fact the perceptiveness to notice what is missing, or not said. Habit is the culprit preventing us from seeing and hearing. Contemporary poets, novelists, musicians, dancers, and artists are superb observers. Their eyes and ears break the barriers to observation that habit creates. John Cage, the twentieth-century experimental composer wrote a piece called 4'33" in which the musicians come on stage without playing a note, and the music that the audience hears is the environment – the sounds they create. "Music is all around us," he said, "if only we have ears to hear" (Cage, 1961). The art of perception is dulled by over familiarity, as medical practitioners in cardiac units know well, from studies of "alarm fatigue" linking overuse of alarms to higher incidences of unheeded cardiac distress (Knox, 2014). Anthropology teaches us to break the barriers that habit creates by looking across cultures. That's when everything is said to be noticeable because it is different and unaccustomed. It sounds like music and looks like art and feels like poetry. A good interview can help find the unfamiliar in the everyday without leaving home.

Observation: Blind because of the unfamiliar

There are limits to perceiving the unfamiliar, however. If there are no cognitive hooks on which to hang new knowledge then sense making is difficult, and it is impossible to distinguish what is meaningful from what is not. Many business anthropologists know the at-sea feeling that characterizes the start of new research in unfamiliar countries, a user-experience study of new technology, or the study of an organization with no org chart. The learning curve is steep, but not impossible. Cognitive and psychological anthropologists have addressed the issues of learning without lattices on which to build and interpret new experiences. Cognitive anthropologist Bradd Shore (Shore 1991: 21) explains that perception depends on what he calls the second birth of an existing cultural model. The first birth is defined by culture and exists in social context, but for the individual to feel comfortable, they need time and motivation to internalize the cultural model. That is the second birth, more commonly called *enculturation*. A cultural model exists twice, once in society and eventually also in the individual. It encodes familiar behavior, complete with belief system and modes of practice. For someone not raised or at least experienced in that cultural environment, perception, understanding, even memory and recall can be flawed or actually impossible until they internalize that model and it becomes part of them. So if a person is lacking a cultural model, they may also be lacking the ability or the desire not only to understand but maybe even to see, as in the mythic story of Meso Americans' inability to "see" Columbus's ships approaching, but for the parting of the waters. (I mention the Meso American image as symbolic of that rich point where we struggle to articulate new cultural knowledge. It was told to me by one of the study participants representing the Tribe whose access to spiritual value in an undisturbed river were at risk because of a licensing request for hydroelectric power. He said you don't understand because you don't have any frame of reference, just like when Columbus's ships approached.)

Defamiliarize the backyard, business implications

I realize that all business anthropology is backyard ethnography in the sense that the collaborators carry stereotypes, subjective biases and opinions, and especially hopes and visions for the product or service for which the research is conducted, not to mention a vested interested in growth and sales. These biases can result in blindspots within the organization about whose perspectives are heard and how and whether the consumer's concerns are reflected. Moreover, the biases and visions of management can result in corporate blindspots about the sourcing of materials (business as usual) and about the supply chain itself including the possibility of bad labor practices and human rights abuses. The deeply examined vignettes and tips for defamiliarizing what is in front of us presented in the "Community Ethnography" section tell us not just that we should take the client to the field and listen to the consumer, but that management and staff within organizations can apply these very tools (frameworks and tips) on themselves as means to unlock "business as usual" and hunt down the assumptions that impeded good business.

Companies of all sizes and in all sectors are challenged to remain relevant to consumers as they are outpaced by changes in the marketplace, say, for example, the shift to mobile and "cloud computing" or the increased relevance of big data and analytics, the role of social media and word-of-mouth marketing. Trends like these require that companies reinvent their brand, transform ways of doing business, create new products. Likewise, shifts in public concerns about the world we live in – sustainability, waste stream reduction and accountability, supply chain and labor conditions. Issues often grouped as Corporate Social Responsibility (CSR) become mandatory for the survival of a brand. To understand what matters to the consumer in changing times and to respond to new marketplace demands with new ways of doing business, some corporations are turning to anthropology and the use of ethnographic methods. Others are taking it upon themselves to restructure according to these changes (for example, the new Microsoft CEO is an expert in cloud computing). A beverage company is considering hiring managers adept in social media because they're plugged in to the consumer, and because it will "free the management team from 'well rehearsed habits'" (Harryson *et al.* 2014: 2). A global advertising firm uses the digital economy as the field of research, creating an "anthropological view" out of snippets plucked from social media to identify a product opportunity (Harrysson *et al.* 2014: 2). Being freed from "well rehearsed habits" is the practice of defamiliarization. As the Harrysson *et al.* article notes, managers who repeat common practices because it is tacitly "known" as the best practice can fall into traps which they indicate can be broken by allying themselves more closely with the consumer point of view by tracking what is posted in the relevant social media. Popular news publications and trade journals have taken note of this kind of anthropological thinking and of the direct role of anthropologists in business (an online search of the key terms *anthropology, ethnography,* and *consumer research* will produce commentary and articles in the likes of *Wired, Atlantic Monthly, McKinsey Quarterly, MIT Sloan Management Review, Harvard Business Review, Financial Times, The Economist, The New Yorker, O! the Oprah Magazine,* and many others).

Conclusions

Though my initial pursuit in examining the vignettes from the Community Ethnography for this chapter was to challenge the limitations of working in familiar settings and to in fact bring to light its benefits, the metaphor of the backyard when extended to environments that are familiar made it clear that people within organizations can internalize ethnographic ways of thinking, and that was seen in the "Client as Ethnographer" discussion when consumers collected anecdotes from friends and family about impressions and knowledge of weatherization experiences, and also in the "Consumer as Ethnographer" section, where clients were often challenged to keep their opinions to themselves and to entertain new models of knowledge about the product that they had. In those circumstances, the "ethnographers" will be faced with the very challenges I was faced with of unearthing our biases and questioning things as if they were unfamiliar. It is with a sense of urgency that I suggest we continue to encourage people in consumer and management research to use the tips and methods identified here to help clients turn the ethnographic lens on themselves and to listen clearly and perceive openly the consumer point of view. With the options proliferating for ways to connect more directly with consumers in business and with management in corporate structure, business anthropology has contributions to make in guiding the ethnographic process even while not controlling every aspect of data collection. The three Community Ethnography cases as well as the "Consumer as Ethnographer" section demonstrate coexistence in a single ethnography of backyard familiarity and defamiliarization, as natural components of perception. Objectivity is not the goal of business ethnography, so the concern with which the chapter opens, of the influences from the participant's position in a community and the constraints from observation in overfamiliar settings and circumstances, are not enough to refrain from bringing the client and the consumer into research, in the increasing modes available.

Acknowledgments

Thanks go to the Ken Erickson for a careful review and for turning me on to a couple of new writers in the backyard ethnography field. Thanks also to Nat Kendall-Turner of the Frameworks Institute, whose excellent and incisive interview structure inspired the writing of this chapter. I alone am responsible for any errors in conveying the theoretical foundations of the interview method. Thanks also to Bruce Tonn, Erin Rose, and Beth Hawkins of ORNL' inspired Weatherization Experience team for the opportunity to help develop and carry out some truly innovative work in anthropology and in the field of consumer side energy knowledge and consumption. I hope to see more work like that from DOE in the future, as it melded knowledge from many sources and integrated recommendations that may, I hope, lead to reduced energy dependency, and to healthier and more comfortable homes across the U.S.

References

Cage, J. (1961). *Silence.* Middleton, CT: Wesleyan University Press.

Cembalest, R. (2012). This Is Not a Pipe–But It IS a Newly Discovered Magritte. *ArtNEWS.*

Clifford, J., & Marcus, G.E. (eds.). (1986). *Writing Culture: The Poetics and Politics of Ethnography.* Berkeley: University of California Press.

Csikszentmihalyi, M. (1990). *Flow: The Psychology of Optimal Experience.* New York, NY: Harper and Row.

Harrysson, M., Métayer, E., & Sarrazin, H. (2014). The strength of 'weak signals.' *McKinsey Quarterly.* www.mckinsey.com/Insights/High_Tech_Telecoms_Inter net/The_strength_of_weak_signals?cid=other-eml-alt-mkq-mck-oth-1402

Holland, D., & Quinn, N. (1987). *Cultural Models in Language & Thought.* Cambridge: Cambridge University Press.

Jackendoff, R. (1985). *Semantics and Cognition.* Cambridge: MIT Press.

Keller, C. M. & Keller, J. D. (1996). *Cognition and Tool Use: The Blacksmith at Work.* Cambridge: Cambridge University Press.

Knox, R. (2014). Silencing Many Hospital Alarms Leads To Better Health Care. www.npr.org/blogs/health/2014/01/24/265702152/silencing-many-hospital-alarms-leads-tobetter-health-care

McLaughlin, E., & Kraus, N. (2003). *The Nanny Diaries: A Novel.* New York: St. Martin's Griffin.

Magritte, R. (1929). Les mots et les images. *La Revolution Surrealiste, 12,* 32–33.

Minsky, M. (1974). A Framework for Representing Knowledge. *MIT-AI Laboratory Memo 306.* Reprinted in Mind Design, J. Haugeland (ed.) (1981). Cambridge: MIT Press. http://web.media.mit.edu/~minsky/papers/Frames/frames.html

Ortlieb, M. (2013). *Introductory remarks to EPIC session, (Co)creation and (Co) participation.* Conference Proceedings of EPIC2013 London. American Anthropological Association.

Peshkin, A. (1988). In Search of Subjectivity – One's Own. *Educational Researcher, 17*(7), 17–21.

Rose, E., & Hawkins, B. (2012). *The Weatherization Experiences Project: Preliminary Findings.* Paper prepared by Oak Ridge National Laboratory, Environmental Sciences Division, as tasked by the United States Department of Energy, presented at The Behavior, Energy, and Climate Change Conference. http://beccconference.org/wp-content/uploads/2012/11/becc_2012_abstracts.pdf

Shore, B. (1991). Twice Born Once Conceived: Meaning Construction and Cultural Cognition. *American Anthropologist, 93*(1), 9–27.

Van Maanen, J. (2011). *Tales of the Field: On Writing Ethnography* (2nd ed.). Chicago: University of Chicago Press.

Von Hippel, E., Ogawa, S., & de Jong, J. P. J. (2011). The Age of the Consumer-Innovator. *MIT Sloan Management Review*, Magazine: Fall 2011. http://sloanreview.mit.edu/article/the-age-of-theconsumer-innovator/

Index

Note: illustrations are denoted by **bold** page numbers, tables by *italic*

For Product Safety Concerns and Information please contact our EU
representative GPSR@taylorandfrancis.com Taylor & Francis Verlag GmbH,
Kaufingerstraße 24, 80331 München, Germany

Printed and bound by CPI Group (UK) Ltd, Croydon, CR0 4YY

01/05/2025

01858425-0001